How to Get Your

America's Foren...
Childcare Experts Answer the Most
Frequently Asked Questions

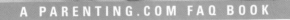

A PARENTING.COM FAQ BOOK

William Sears, M.D., and Martha Sears, R.N.

Look for all four Parenting.com FAQ books by William Sears, M.D., and Martha Sears, R.N.

Clear, concise, reliable answers to the questions that parents most frequently ask

Look in the back of this book for information about the Sears Parenting Library, the bestselling parenting guides for a new generation.

Little, Brown and Company
Available wherever books are sold

The First Three Months

William Sears, M.D., and Martha Sears, R.N.

0-316-77668-8

How to Get Your Baby to Sleep

William Sears, M.D., and Martha Sears, R.N.

0-316-77620-3

Keeping Your Baby Healthy

William Sears, M.D., and Martha Sears, R.N.

0-316-77680-7

Feeding the Picky Eater

William Sears, M.D., and Martha Sears, R.N.

0-316-77671-7

WILLIAM SEARS, M.D., and MARTHA SEARS, R.N., are the pediatrics experts to whom American parents are increasingly turning for advice and information on all aspects of pregnancy, birth, childcare, and family nutrition. Dr. Sears was trained at Harvard Medical School's Children's Hospital and Toronto's Hospital for Sick Children, the largest children's hospital in the world. He has practiced pediatrics for nearly thirty years and currently serves as a medical and parenting consultant to *Baby Talk* and *Parenting* magazines. Martha Sears is a registered nurse, certified childbirth educator, and breastfeeding consultant. The Searses are the parents of eight children.

More information about the Searses can be found at www.SearsParenting.com and www.AskDrSears.com.

How to Get Your Baby to Sleep

America's Foremost Baby and
Childcare Experts Answer the Most
Frequently Asked Questions

William Sears, M.D.,
and Martha Sears, R.N.

Little, Brown and Company
BOSTON | NEW YORK | LONDON

First Edition

The information herein is not intended to replace the services of trained health professionals. You are advised to consult with your child's health-care professional with regard to matters relating to your child's health, and in particular matters that may require diagnosis or medical attention.

Library of Congress Cataloging-in-Publication Data

Sears, William, M.D.
    How to get your baby to sleep / William Sears and Martha Sears — 1st ed.
      p. cm.
    Includes index.
    ISBN 0-316-77620-3
    1. Infants — Sleep. 2. Child care. 3. Children — Sleep.
I. Sears, Martha. II. Title.
RJ506.S55 S425 2001
649'.1 — dc21   00-045645

10 9 8 7 6 5 4 3 2 1

Printed in the United States of America

Book design and text composition by L&G McRee

Introduction

During the more than thirty years we have spent coun-
seling thousands of moms and dads in nighttime parenting—not to mention the many nights we have spent
lulling our own eight children to sleep—we have developed many time-tested techniques and principles for
coaxing babies and toddlers into slumber. We've learned,
as we share throughout this book, that effective nighttime
parenting is more about maintaining conditions conducive
to sleep than trying the latest sleep fads.

So how can you nurture good sleep habits with your
baby? The best way to start is to develop a practical sleep
strategy. As you may know, babies rarely sleep through the
night for the first six months (except your friends' babies,
of course!). And let's not forget that you cannot force your
baby to sleep any more than you can force her to eat.

Your parenting goal is to encourage your baby to
develop a healthy attitude about sleep. This is done by creating an environment in which sleep naturally overtakes
your baby. This way she will feel comfortable falling
asleep and remaining asleep on her own—not just now, but
as she gets older—and avoid many of the sleep problems
experienced by older children and adults who never
manage to develop a healthy sleep attitude on their own.

This book differs from the usual sleep-training books,
which are variations of the same old tired theme: Let baby
cry it out. This insensitive method of sleep training offers

a short-term solution that actually results in a long-term loss. Simply put, it's a bad investment. Of course you can put cotton in your ears and let baby cry alone in a crib— baby will go to sleep eventually. But we want your child to grow up with a healthy sleep attitude—to regard sleep as a pleasant state to enter and a fearless state in which to remain. That is why we promote nighttime parenting, an approach that helps your child grow up with a peaceful attitude about sleep and a trusting attitude about his parents, who have helped him enjoy sleep.

In this book, we give you practical tools to help your baby develop good sleep habits. We look at a variety of situations that may make nighttime parenting more challenging, such as night nursing after Mom returns to work. We also look at conditions that may trigger night waking. Don't forget that the early, high-maintenance restless months and sleepless nights do not go on forever. The time you spend rocking or nursing your baby to sleep, comforting her in the middle of a night waking, and experimenting with various sleep arrangements to find the best one is a short period in a total life span. But the memories of nighttime parental trust will last forever!

WILLIAM SEARS, M.D., and MARTHA SEARS, R.N.

How to Get Your Baby to Sleep

Getting Days and Nights
Mixed Up

Q *Help! My newborn came home from the hospital with her days and nights mixed up. We have no clue how to reverse this. My husband and I alternate nights walking the hallway while baby is wide-eyed, alert, and cooing. Surely you have some sleep secrets to share!*

A Wouldn't it be wonderful to have a menu of tips and tricks you could try until you hit upon a magic antidote to end baby's restless nights? There are no special secrets in this book. Instead, we will show you how to adopt realistic sleep goals for you and your baby.

Many babies come into the world with their sleep-wake cycle established. In utero they slept when Mom was awake, and they were awake when Mom went to sleep. As parents you need to teach your infant that daytime is for feeding and interacting, and nighttime is for sleeping—not the reverse.

Here's how to change your baby's sleep-wake cycle: During the day, wake your baby for feedings so that she does not sleep longer than three hours at a stretch. Play with her after each feeding for as long as she can stay awake, and keep her with you in a stimulating environment. At night, keep things calm and quiet—low lights, quiet music, soft voices, and minimal stimulation. When your baby awakens at night, respond to her quickly, but in a no-nonsense mode (keep talking to a minimum and use a night-light to see by).

The message you want to send is that you expect your baby to fall asleep. You may have read that some babies can be put down to sleep while they are still awake and they will settle themselves off to sleep. In reality most babies do not have this type of sleep temperament. Most babies need to be "parented" to sleep—not just put down to sleep—and this means they need to be rocked and nursed.

In normal sleep development, you will find that as the months go by, your baby's stretches of daytime sleep will automatically shorten, and her nighttime sleep will lengthen.

✑

What "Sleeping Through the Night" Really Means

Q *Our pediatrician continues to use the phrase "sleeping through the night." I hate to sound silly, but what does that really mean? Is it eight hours? Five hours?*

A "Sleeping through the night" has a different meaning for different babies and their parents, and the amount of uninterrupted sleep at night varies greatly from baby to baby. In sleep studies "sleeping through the night," or "settling," is defined as a five-hour stretch, at least in the first few months. To expect a baby to sleep from 8:00 P.M. to 8:00 A.M. is totally unrealistic for most babies. Having a baby under six months who sleeps longer than a five-hour stretch at night is a luxury rather than a right.

Early in your parenting career, you will realize that the only baby who sleeps through the night in the early months is someone else's baby. The age at which babies sleep through the night varies tremendously and is usually a reflection of your baby's temperament and not your nighttime parenting skills.

By three to four months of age, most babies reward their parents with a longer period of sleep at night. In a sleep study of a large group of infants, 70 percent of babies slept five-hour stretches by three months; 13 percent slept five-hour stretches by six months; and 10 percent of babies did not sleep for five-hour stretches until one year.

☙

Nothing Seems to Work!

Q *I am supposed to go back to work in two weeks, and my baby still has not developed a normal nighttime routine. Is there anything I can do to speed this up? I want both of us to feel rested.*

A It is important to consider the time and effort you spend helping your baby sleep as a long-term investment in her sleep future—and it does take time and effort. You can help nurture her good sleep habits by trying the following:

- *Experiment with different sleep styles.* Babies have different sleep temperaments, and families have different needs and lifestyles. You may need to experiment with several methods to find a sleep style that suits both your baby's and your family's needs. If you and your infant are both getting enough sleep (well, almost enough), then your style of nighttime parenting is right for you. If you aren't, try something else. Be prepared for a sleep style to lose its effectiveness as baby grows and her needs change.

- *Introduce a variety of sleep associations.* Everyone, babies and adults alike, wakes up several times each night. Most adults drift back to sleep on their own without realizing that they have awoken at all. Babies, on the other hand, may need help getting back to sleep and may expect the same parental involvement each time. This means that if you consistently rock or nurse your baby to sleep each night at 9:00 P.M., she may expect this when she awakens at midnight, 2:00 A.M., and 5:00 A.M. So introduce a variety of ways to help her get to sleep. Sometimes you may nurse her to sleep, but other times rock her or sing to her as she drifts off to sleep. Alternate by using tape recordings to help her relax. Also, trade off with your spouse so you are not the only one who can successfully lull her to sleep. It is important that babies get used to Dad's comforting style so that he can put baby down to sleep—and back to sleep. Otherwise, Mom may suffer from burnout. Dad's contribution is especially important for the breastfed infant, who is likely to assume that "Mom's diner" is open twenty-four hours a day. (For suggestions on preparing baby for sleep see page 51.)

- *Tank up your baby during the day.* Babies need to learn that nighttime is for sleeping, and daytime is for eating. Some older babies and toddlers are so busy playing during the day that they forget to eat. Then when nighttime comes, they want to make up for lost meals. Try to feed your baby at least every three hours during the day so that she's sure to get her fill before bedtime. When she wakes the first time during the night, attempt a full feeding. Otherwise, some infants, particularly those being breastfed, will want to nibble all night.

- *Beware of sleep trainers.* From the moment the first parenting book landed in the nursery, infant-sleep experts have been claiming that they can help parents train babies to sleep better with a simple step-by-step procedure. Unfortunately, most sleep-training techniques are just variations of the old "let baby cry it out" method. This antiquated approach has three strikes against it.

First, it undermines the trust and confidence your baby places in you for her nighttime comfort and safety. Your baby counts on you to provide everything she needs in life: warmth, food, comfort, and safety. How secure would your baby feel if she couldn't trust you to come when she called? Babies rarely cry for no reason. Second, it prevents you from developing a nighttime parenting style that best addresses the needs of you and your baby. There is no "one size fits all" sleep style. Every baby (and parent) is unique. And third, it may keep you and your doctor from discovering potential medical reasons for your baby's night waking.

In working out your sleep techniques and rituals, be sensitive to the nighttime needs of your baby. Remember your ultimate goal: to encourage a healthy sleep attitude without robbing yourself or anyone else in your family of needed rest.

Mom vs. Machine

What will they think of next? There are all kinds of new gizmos on the market these days: oscillating cradles, crib vibrators, teddy bears that "breathe"—each one designed to lull a baby to sleep, no parents necessary. Somehow we can't help but feel that human touch counts for something, and we are quite sure baby would agree.

Infants and children sleep better and grow better when they are on the receiving end of a loving touch. Health-care providers have long known that children who are touched a lot grow better and behave better. Now research shows that babies receiving extra touch, such as being held for long periods during the day, sleep better at night. Touch settles babies and helps them relax. In addition to the research, common sense tells us that babies prefer Mom to machines.

Put yourself behind the eyes of a baby. Would you want to sleep in a dark, quiet room, being lulled to sleep by a vibrating crib? Or would you prefer nestling next to your favorite person in the whole wide world, enjoying the warmth of her body, the instant touch when needed, and even your favorite nighttime pleasure, nursing? This is something no machine can even come close to providing.

The importance of touch has been recognized for decades. One of the oldest treatments for "failure to thrive," the medical term for babies who are not growing well, is to take the baby to bed and nurse. There's something special about a mother's touch that helps babies thrive. Remember, thriving means more than growing or getting taller and heavier. Thriving means growing optimally—intellectually, physically, and emotionally. A nurturing style of nighttime parenting helps babies thrive.

⬿

A Safe Sleeping Environment

Q *We are getting the nursery ready for our first baby and are looking to purchase a new crib. What do you recommend in a safe crib and bedding?*

A Crib and bedding accidents, such as suffocating between a poorly fitting mattress and the crib, are among the leading causes of death in infants under a year. Here are some guidelines to help you give your baby the safest sleep environment possible:

• Buy a crib with a label from either the U.S. Consumer Product Safety Commission (CPSC) or the Juvenile Products Manufacturers Association (JPMA) stating that it conforms to their safety standards.

• Measure the spaces between the bars of the crib rails to be sure they aren't more than 2⅜ inches (6 centimeters) apart. Larger gaps, often found in cribs manufactured before 1979, make it possible for baby to get her head caught between the bars.

• Make sure that the mattress fits the crib perfectly. Undersize mattresses leave spaces on the sides or the ends of the crib where an infant's head can get caught and cause suffocation. Push the mattress to one corner of the crib and check that any resulting spaces aren't bigger than 1½ inches (4 centimeters). If you can fit more than two fingers between the mattress and the crib, the mattress is too small. Beware of secondhand cribs, which may come with a different mattress from the original one that was designed to fit the crib exactly.

- Beware of mattresses that are too soft and can be easily pushed away from the side of the crib. In fact, don't put your baby down to sleep on any soft surface. The wrinkles and crevices found in water beds, beanbags, and other squishy surfaces can trap stale air against baby's face and obstruct his breathing.

- Inspect the crib's mattress support system periodically. Rattle the metal hangers and push down on the mattress from above, then up from underneath. Any hanger that comes out of place needs to be fixed or replaced. The hangers supporting the mattress and support board should be secured in their notches by safety clips.

- Make sure that the crib bumpers fit snugly around the entire perimeter of the crib and are secured with ties or snaps. Trim the excess length from bumper ties to keep your baby from chewing on them or getting entangled in them. Similarly, check toys, mobiles, pacifiers, and bedding to be sure they have no strings more than 7 inches (17.5 centimeters) long on which baby can choke.

- Spread top sheets and fitted sheets as smoothly as possible and tuck them in tightly beneath the mattress to lessen the chance of wrinkles developing in the bedding, which could obstruct a baby's breathing. Don't use loose-fitting plastic mattress covers or waterproof sheets that can wrap around a baby's head and cause suffocation. Top sheets and blankets should be large enough that you can firmly tuck them under the sides and end at baby's feet. Still, don't tuck baby's covers so tightly as to restrict his freedom of movement.

- Remove the bumpers and toys from baby's crib once he can pull himself up, usually between seven and nine months. You do not want him stepping on these to climb over the crib railing. Also, don't attach crib toys between the side rails or hang them over the crib after baby is old enough to push up on hands and knees (usually about five months). Older babies can easily become entangled in the dangling cords or use the toys to climb over the crib railing.

- Keep baby's environment as fuzz-free as possible. If your infant is susceptible to respiratory allergies, use hypoallergenic mattresses and mattress covers. Avoid putting stuffed animals, which collect lint, dust, and hair, in baby's crib. Also, avoid fuzzy wool bedding and deep-pile lambskins. Not only do they attract allergens, but they can obstruct baby's breathing passages.

- Choose the placement of your baby's crib with care. It should not be near a heater or any dangling cords from blinds or draperies. Nor should it be placed against a window or close to any furniture that your baby could use to climb out of the crib by reaching through the crib bars to gain a foot- or handhold. Give some thought to what could happen if your baby did manage to climb out. His crib should be situated so that he wouldn't fall against any sharp objects or get trapped, or even strangled, between the crib and an adjacent wall or piece of furniture.

- Don't leave your sleeping baby unattended around other children, who may lovingly but unwisely want to nestle a teddy bear next to baby's head. If your baby's crib isn't within hearing distance of every room in the house, use a portable baby monitor to keep an ear out for strange noises or silences.

- When spending the night away from home, keep in mind that hotel rooms and relatives' homes are never as baby friendly as your own home. Travel with a portable crib or a roll-out safe-sleeping mat that is at least 1 inch (2.5 centimeters) thick. These are safer alternatives than the soft mattresses typically found on sofa beds or motel rollaways. If you use a crib furnished by a hotel, inspect it as described above.

- Be equally vigilant when putting baby to sleep in a carriage. Carriage mattresses tend to be less cared for than other bedding. Clean the baby carriage mattress regularly to keep it free from dust and other allergens. Also, keep baby's carriage clear of stuffed animals and pillows. Carriages are second only to cribs as the most common settings for smothering.

- Use caution if you try to jury-rig your own bedside co-sleeper, which is a criblike infant bed that attaches to the side of your bed. Co-sleepers put a baby within arm's reach of Mom, close enough for easy touching and nursing. At the same time, they give babies their own sleeping space. Many parents put the baby's crib next to their own bed instead of purchasing a safe co-sleeper. Some even remove the crib's side rail so that the crib becomes an extension of their mattress. Unfortunately, the crib can move away from the side of the bed, leaving a gap in which baby can be trapped or through which he can fall. It's safer to purchase a co-sleeper that attaches flush with the adult mattress. We recommend the Arm's

Reach Co-Sleeper. See Resources for Childcare Products and Information, page 103.

- For more suggestions on ways to reduce the likelihood of crib accidents, order a crib safety pamphlet from the U.S. Consumer Product Safety Commission (800-638-2772; www.cpsc.gov). Crib safety advice is also available from the Juvenile Products Manufacturers Association. Send a self-addressed, stamped envelope to JPMA, 236 Route 38 West, Suite 100, Moorestown, NJ 08057, or go to their Web site at www.jpma.org. In Canada, a crib safety pamphlet is available from Health Canada, Product Safety Resources (613-957-3143; www.hc-sc.gc.ca/ehp/ehd/psb). Write to Publishing Unit, Environmental Health Directorate, Health Canada, A.L. 0801A, Ottawa, ON K1A 0L2.

Bedtime Sleepwear

Q *What is the best sleepwear for a baby? How warmly should my baby be dressed at night?*

A Dressing your baby appropriately is really only a matter of common sense and getting a feel for your individual baby. Unless your baby was born prematurely, weighs less than 8 pounds, or lacks some typical insulating fat (a condition your doctor would call being small for date), dressing him too warmly could be unsafe.

New insights into infant sleep show that overheating can lull a baby into a deep sleep that is hard to rouse from. This inability to easily arouse from sleep is linked to Sudden Infant Death Syndrome (SIDS), which is the primary cause of death in infants between one month and one year, with peak incidences around three months of age. To help prevent SIDS, the American Academy of Pediatrics recently cautioned parents not to overheat their babies' sleeping environment, particularly if the infant is less than six months old. Here are some tips that will keep baby safe:

- Don't cover baby's head with any kind of hood or cap during the first week. This is your baby's primary path of body heat loss. (Very premature hospitalized babies often need their head covered to maintain their body temperature, but the medical staff will monitor this.)

- If you share your bed with your baby, pay special attention to your baby's body temperature. A co-sleeping baby shares his parents' body warmth as well as their bed and can easily become overheated.

- Make it a habit to monitor your infant's body temperature. Touch her head or the back of her neck. If these areas feel too hot or if your baby is sweating or her hair is damp, remove one layer of clothing. If your baby feels cold, add a layer. Overall, it's safer to adjust baby's sleeping temperature by changing her clothes than by piling on more blankets.

- Don't use your baby's hands and feet as indicators of body temperature. In most babies, these parts are usually cooler than the rest of the body. You should keep your baby's bedroom at 68° to 70° F, with a relative humidity of about 60 to 70 percent.

- If you change baby's sleeping arrangements, adjust her sleepwear accordingly. For example, if you dress baby for sleeping in a crib in her bedroom and then take her into your bed after the first waking, you may need to take off a layer of clothing because of the increased warmth from your body.

- When choosing both baby's sleepwear and your own, avoid clothes with dangling strings or ties; they present a risk of strangulation or choking. Remove any attached objects (decorative buttons, for example, or bows that could come untied) that might also cause strangulation or choking. Also, we recommend flame-retardant cotton clothing because it absorbs body moisture and allows air to circulate freely.

There are two types of sleepwear for infants: footed sleepers and loose, tie-at-the-bottom sacques. Sleepers that cover a baby's feet are the most practical. Even if baby kicks off his blankets, you can be sure he still has at least one layer of warmth. A minor drawback to sleepers is that it's harder to get a good fit in a one-piece garment. Still, they don't need to fit perfectly. Your baby's sleepwear should be loose-fitting enough to allow free movement yet close-fitting enough that his arms and legs stay inside the clothes. It won't take you long to figure out which your baby likes better, a footed sleeper or a sacque.

- Use a single, porous blanket for crib sleepers. Avoid heavy comforters, which don't breathe. To keep baby from sliding under the covers, tuck the bottom portion of the covers tightly beneath baby's feet. Or place baby so his feet touch the lower end of the crib. Tuck the blanket snugly beneath each side of the crib mattress, but don't fit the blanket so tightly as to restrict baby's freedom of movement.

- If your baby likes to "sleep tight," swaddle her. This means snugly wrap baby in a soft receiving blanket. Both experience and research have shown that swaddled babies sleep longer, especially babies who startle themselves easily by their random, jerky movements. Swaddling contains these babies and reminds them of the close confines of the womb. New insights have prompted orthopedists to discourage swaddling newborns because it may interfere with proper development of the hips. For this reason it's wise not to swaddle your baby all night every night.

Arms-free swaddling is the least restrictive and the safest. Also, take extra care to place your baby to sleep on his back and to leave his head uncovered. While back-sleeping is a safe sleeping position for most babies, it's especially imperative for bundled-up babies who won't have as much freedom of movement to adjust the position of their face against the mattress.

❧

Sleeping in a Noisy House

Q *I have a new baby as well as two children ages six and four. My house is always noisy. Must my baby have quiet to sleep?*

A Babies can sleep quite well in a noisy environment. The womb, a baby's very first sleeping space, is a surprisingly loud place, mostly because of the noise of the blood flow through the womb vessels. Yet babies sleep through it all.

In fact, babies become so accustomed to the sounds of the womb that recordings of these sounds have been used as infant sleep aids for years. The humming sounds of the modern household—vacuum cleaners, air conditioners, and dishwashers—also make effective lullabies for baby. These monotonous, repetitious sounds basically bore the baby to sleep.

As parents of eight, we can say that our babies got as much sleep as they needed in our sometimes tumultuous home. Most babies simply have an innate talent for tuning out disruptive noises as they retreat into a deep sleep.

However, not all babies are alike. If your little one is easily awakened by the laughter and screams of playing children, teach your older children to respect "quiet time" while baby is sleeping. You can make this part of a larger lesson on respect for others' needs. Have older children play outside or in a room distant from the sleeping baby. Encourage more quiet play, or perhaps arrange for baby's naptime to be their "video time."

When boisterous noise is unavoidable, play music just loud enough to drown out the ambient noise of the household. The steady rhythms, even at a low volume, should lull baby back to sleep.

❧

The Perfect Place for Baby

Q *My husband and I differ on where our baby should sleep. Because she startles easily when she hears a noise, my husband prefers that she sleep in a crib in her bedroom. On nights when she is extremely fussy, I put her in a small cradle in our bedroom or even in our bed. My husband firmly believes that she should not sleep between us. Yet I want to respond quickly to her needs. How can we get her to sleep longer and still get the rest we need to function the next day?*

A You cannot force a baby to sleep. You can only foster an environment in which sleep naturally overtakes your baby. Keep in mind that there is no one right place for babies to sleep. The best sleep arrangement is the one that allows members of your family to get the most sleep. For example, one baby might sleep best in a crib in her own room. Another might sleep best in a bassinet or crib in her parents' bedroom. Another baby might sleep best snuggled next to Mommy in her parents' bed or in a co-sleeper, as described on page 12.

Once you have chosen the best place for your baby to sleep, consider ways to make sleep more attractive to her. The effectiveness of each tactic may depend on your baby's stage of development, and what doesn't work one week may work the next.

- *Work on daytime mellowing.* A peaceful night is usually preceded by a peaceful day, as the quiet calm laps over into baby's sleep. When your baby has a restless night, ask yourself if there were any elements that might have disturbed her day. Were you too busy to handle her patiently? Did she spend enough time in the arms of a caring adult? Was she mainly confined to her crib? We have found that babies who are held or worn in a carrier, especially the sling type, for several hours during the day cry less overall and settle down better at night.

- *Adopt a consistent naptime routine.* Babies with consistent nap routines during the day are more likely to sleep for longer stretches at night. Predictable nap schedules usually make for a relaxing, stress-reduced day for baby. A stress-free day usually means easier sleeping at night.

  Select a couple of times during the day when you are most tired, say, 11:00 A.M. and 4:00 P.M. Lie down with baby every day for a week at these times. This should be enough to establish this daytime nap schedule in your child's mind, and it will serve to let you get some much-needed rest. Remember to sleep when baby sleeps. Don't waste these precious quiet moments on housework.

- *Give her consistent bedtimes.* Babies with consistent bedtimes, as well as bedtime routines, usually fall asleep more easily and stay asleep longer. When a child goes to sleep at the same time every night, her internal clock adapts, making it easier for her to drift off to dreamland promptly.

  Remember, time spent with Mom and Dad is prime

time, and your baby will milk it for all it's worth. In these cases, a later afternoon nap and a later bedtime may work best for all.

- *Establish a bedtime routine.* Like regular bedtimes, familiar bedtime rituals help babies learn when it is time for bed. These daily routines get them started in the transition from being awake to being asleep. A warm bath followed by a soothing massage helps to relax baby's tense muscles and busy mind. (Be careful, though, because this can stimulate some babies.) Rocking, nursing, and lullabies also capitalize on "patterns of association." This is an important trait of early infant behavior that allows baby to recognize the start of the bedtime routine and anticipate the finale—*sleep!* Babies can get used to multiple routines, and there is good reason not to go with just one (see page 6).

ᧈ

Sleeping with Pets

Q *We have a cat that likes to curl up with us at night. Should we put a stop to this when the baby comes?*

A If you choose to sleep with baby in your bed, the kitty must find a new place to nap. Once your cat sees that baby is curled up next to you in its favorite sleeping spot, it will probably want to nestle right next to baby to reclaim its space. If your cat curls up against baby's face, its fur could obstruct her breathing. Also, animal dander—cat, dog, or any other kind—can irritate a newborn's sensitive nasal passages, causing congestion and making it difficult to breathe. Never allow pets to sleep in baby's crib.

When your child reaches toddlerhood (twelve to eighteen months), pets may become welcome and safe sleep partners if there are no allergies. In some cases your child's furry friend will act as an attachment object that can result in a more restful night's sleep.

⟋⟍

Newborn Breathing Can
Alter Sleep

Q *Our three-week-old sounds as if her nose is stuffy all the time. I think this keeps her from sleeping soundly. Is there anything I should do?*

A Older babies can breathe easily through their mouths if their noses are blocked, but for infants mouth-breathing is difficult, so it is important to keep their nasal passages clear during their first few months. An allergy to something in your baby's sleeping environment can cause a stuffy nose and a buildup of fluid behind the eardrums, making it difficult for her to sleep. Bedroom inhalant allergies are common causes of stuffy noses and consequent night waking. Keep your baby's bedroom as dust-free as possible by cleaning it regularly and removing fuzzy blankets, down comforters, and dust-collecting furry stuffed animals and toys.

If your baby is particularly allergy-prone, a HEPA-type air filter will help reduce the allergens in the air. HEPA filters are efficient in filtering out almost 100 percent of airborne allergens and danders and are available at most allergy-supply centers.

☙

The Ideal Room Temperature for Sleeping

Q *My husband and I have an ongoing debate about the best room temperature for our infant son. Which is better—warm or cool?*

A Temperature is important in developing good sleep habits for baby. In fact, placing a warm baby on cold cotton sheets can undo most of your sleep-inducing efforts. In cold weather, use flannel sheets or warm the sheets with a heated towel before laying baby down.

As far as room temperature goes, babies prefer a consistent bedroom temperature of around 70° F and a relative humidity of 60 to 70 percent.

❧

What to Do When Baby Wakes

Q *When our first two children were infants, they hardly ever woke up when I put them to bed. But our third child wakes up several times during the night. I've tried everything from nursing her to sleep to infant massage to letting her cry. None of these work effectively. Is there another option? I'm exhausted!*

A Dealing with night waking is the most energy-zapping nighttime parenting task. Some babies are natural self-soothers, able to resettle easily and quickly without much help. But most need a helping hand, breast, or whatever else you can muster up at 3:00 A.M. Many of the transitioning techniques on page 51 are applicable here.

A tactic that has worked for many bleary-eyed parents is one we call "the laying on of hands." If your baby sleeps in your bed, you can probably sense when she is stirring, on the verge of awakening. When that happens, you can head off a full-blown night waking by touching her firmly with your palms. Remove your hands gradually—first one, and then the other—easing the pressure slowly so as not to startle baby awake. That simple physical assurance that you are there may be enough to send her back to dreamland. Sometimes fathers, perhaps because they have larger hands, are more successful with this hands-on ritual. It helps to pat your baby's back or bottom rhythmically in time with your heartbeat. (To learn more about the benefits of sleep-sharing, turn to page 36.)

If you've tried it all and your infant is waking frequently in a manner that suggests she may be in pain, discuss the following possible medical causes with your doctor. You might suspect a medical cause particularly if she is "colicky" during the day.

Gastroesophageal Reflux

Gastroesophageal reflux (GER) is one of the most common medical causes of night waking (and colicky behavior). GER stems from a weakness in the circular band of muscle where the esophagus joins the stomach. Irritating stomach acids are regurgitated into baby's esophagus, causing pain similar to heartburn. Symptoms include the following:

- painful bursts of night waking
- fussiness, particularly after eating
- frequent spitting up (although not all babies with GER spit up regularly)
- frequent bouts of colicky, abdominal pain
- bouts of unexplained wheezing
- throaty sounds after feeding

Teething Pain

Teething pain, even though you may not yet be able to feel your baby's teeth, can start as early as three months. It may persist on and off right up to the appearance of the two-

year molars. Look for the following signs that teething
pain is keeping your baby up at night:

- a wet bed sheet under baby's head
- a drool rash on baby's cheeks and chin
- swollen and tender gums
- a slight fever

With your doctor's permission, administer appropriate
doses of acetaminophen just before bed and again in four
hours if baby wakes up.

Dairy Allergies

Dairy allergies, either to a milk-based formula or dairy
products in a breastfeeding mother's diet, will also keep a
baby from sleeping. Symptoms include:

- bloating
- diarrhea
- a red rash around the baby's anus
- many of the symptoms prevalent in GER (see above)

☙

Do Big Babies Sleep Better?

Q *My best friend's baby is the same age as my two-month-old and weighs 3 pounds more. While my baby still demands to be fed at least once during the night, her baby sleeps seven hours at a time. My friend is rested, and I'm exhausted. Is it true that big babies sleep better at night?*

A Not necessarily. There are several factors that affect how long a baby sleeps. It may depend on baby's maturity, for instance. Premature babies have a higher percentage of active sleep, causing them to sleep more lightly. This may be a survival mechanism with developmental benefits for the growing baby. Premature babies need approximately 25 percent more nutrition for catch-up growth, so consequently, preterm babies may awaken to feed more often. The same is true for small-for-date babies (those born with a diminished reserve of body fat). Plump babies with extra body fat may have extra reserves to tide them over, so they tend to awaken less frequently for feedings.

Besides maturity, the temperament of a baby influences night waking. Mellow babies usually carry their laid-back personalities into their sleep and may awaken less easily. Active or "hyper" babies may be so stimulated by their environment that they have more difficulty sleeping.

Also, the maturity of baby's digestive system can influence night waking. Infants with immature intestinal development, due to food allergies and/or gastroesophageal reflux (see page 23), for example, may awaken more frequently because of intestinal upsets.

Finally, breastfed infants awaken to feed more frequently largely because breast milk is digested more quickly than formula.

Remember, too, that sleeping longer does not always mean sleeping safer. See page 29.

☞

Why Is My Infant Such a Light Sleeper?

Q *My baby is such a light sleeper. When I finally do get her to sleep, she sometimes wakes up as soon as I put her down. She also wakes up crying several times in the middle of the night. I know this is not unusual for babies, but isn't there something I can do?*

A Nearly everything babies do they do for a certain reason. That includes sleeping during the day, sleeping for only a few hours at a time, and even waking up at 3:00 A.M. All of these are necessary for your baby's mental and physical development. To deal with these seemingly erratic sleeping habits, you must understand the difference between a baby in deep sleep and a baby in light sleep.

Before we explore that difference let's review some facts about adult sleep. When you first drift off to sleep, your higher brain center slows down, enabling you to enter non-REM (non-rapid-eye-movement) sleep. This is considered deep sleep. Your body is still. Your breathing is shallow, and your muscles are loose. You're really zonked.

After an hour and a half of non-REM sleep, your brain begins to wake up. You move from deep sleep into a light, or active, sleep called REM (rapid-eye-movement) sleep. During this sleep stage, you dream and might turn over or even adjust the covers without fully awakening. You might even wake up completely to go to the bathroom or get a drink of water. These cycles of light and deep sleep alternate very couple of hours throughout the night, adding up to an average of six hours of deep sleep and two hours of light, active sleep.

Babies sleep differently from adults. Whereas adults can usually go directly into non-REM, deep sleep, infants go through an initial period of REM, active sleep that lasts for about twenty minutes before they gradually drift into a deep sleep. This is why your baby wakes up if you put her down too soon. Many parents have told me, "My baby has to be fully asleep before I can put her down."

As they mature, babies learn to pass more quickly through the light sleep stage and enter deep sleep. Until then, you need to learn to recognize your baby's sleep stages so you know when it's best to move her from one sleeping place to another. For example, she should be sleeping deeply before you move her from your bed or from a car seat to her crib.

On a typical night you will rock, walk, or nurse your baby. While her eyes are closed, her eyelids may flutter and her breathing will be irregular. Her hands and limbs will be flexed, and she may startle, twitch, and bless you with some fleeting smiles called sleep grins. If you lay her down at this point, she'll wake up because she is in a light, active sleep.

If you extend your bedtime ritual about twenty minutes longer, your baby's grimaces and twitches will stop, her breathing will become more regular and shallow, and her muscles will completely relax. Her clenched hands will unfold and her limbs will droop weightlessly, giving what Martha and I call the "limp-limb" sign of deep sleep. Now it is safe to put your baby down and sneak away, knowing that she's finally resting comfortably.

Throughout the night, infants alternate between light and deep sleep more frequently than adults do. Your infant is more likely to awaken during the period of active sleep if she is hungry, her diaper is wet, or if she hears a loud noise. If she doesn't awaken, after about ten minutes she will descend back into a deep sleep. An hour later, she will enter light sleep again and be more likely to awaken for about ten minutes.

Just like your own sleep cycle, this cycle continues throughout the night. Yet because your baby enters active sleep more often than you do—as often as once an hour— she's more likely to wake up during the night. Besides having more vulnerable periods, some babies have trouble making the transition from light sleep back to deep sleep and need a helping hand, voice, or breast.

Most bleary-eyed parents find it incredibly unfair that nature has designed an infant sleep cycle so much more delicate and accelerated than an adult's. Nonetheless, it keeps your baby safer and stimulates mental development. Knowing these facts may help you feel better about the sleep you've sacrificed and encourage you to develop a strategy that best serves your baby's nighttime needs.

Smart Sleep

Q *I read something about how light sleep helps to make a baby smart. What does this mean?*

A Light sleep is smart sleep. Sleep researchers call light sleep active sleep. In contrast to deep, or non-REM sleep, the brain is not at rest in active sleep but is partially awake and active. During light sleep, your infant's body pumps more blood to the brain and increases its production of nerve proteins for brain growth. (I once mentioned this light-sleep brain growth to a mother in my practice, and she responded, "Then my baby will be very smart!")

Sleep researchers believe that it is during light, or active, sleep that a substantial amount of learning is done. We think that the brain processes much of the information collected during our waking hours, storing what it thinks is important while discarding what may not be important. Some researchers theorize that active sleep stimulates a baby's developing brain, providing visual imagery to promote mental development. The lower brain centers fire off electrical impulses at the higher brain centers to get them to react and develop.

Light sleep is also safer sleep. Babies have more constant, demanding physical needs than do their parents. While you can afford to sleep in a room that is too hot or too cold or to sleep with hunger that has developed during the night, your infant cannot. If baby slept like you, with more deep than active sleep, she might miss the nutrition, warmth, and comfort she needs to grow and thrive.

While rare, Sudden Infant Death Syndrome (SIDS) is a danger to your infant's well-being. With its stimulation of baby's breathing centers, I believe that active sleep is nature's defense against the stop-breathing episodes that can cause SIDS. It helps wake baby up if she has trouble breathing. (For more about the dangers of SIDS and reducing your baby's risk, see the next page.)

Frequent active sleep cycles are wired into infants so that they will wake up if circumstances threaten their well-being. Of course, you need your sleep, too. Turn to page 54 for safe ways to get your baby to sleep longer at night.

Did You Know?

Premature babies spend approximately 90 percent of their sleep time in active, REM sleep as opposed to the 50 to 70 percent of active sleep time experienced by full-term babies. The purpose may be to accelerate their brain growth and make up for lost womb time. Or it could be that the younger the baby, the more active sleep she needs. The fetus may experience nearly 100 percent active sleep. Two-year-olds get 25 percent active sleep, while adolescents and adults receive about 20 percent. We believe that the more rapid the brain development, the greater the percentage of active versus deep sleep.

Sudden Infant Death Syndrome

Q *Can you tell me more about SIDS? I am pregnant for the first time, and I don't want this to happen to me. What can I do to make sure my baby doesn't become a SIDS victim?*

A Each year approximately three thousand babies in the United States go to sleep and never wake up. No one knows why. While SIDS occurs in only one out of every one thousand babies, this tragedy ranks near the top of every parent's worry list.

Nevertheless, there is good news. Recent research strongly suggests a number of preventive measures parents can take to lower the risk and worry of SIDS. These risk-reduction measures enhance a baby's pre- and postnatal development, promote respiratory health, and increase parental awareness of a baby's needs—any one of which may reduce the likelihood of SIDS.

Provide a Healthy Womb Environment

Premature birth and low birth weight are two of the highest risk factors for SIDS. To give your baby the best prenatal start:

- Get good prenatal care. Babies whose mothers receive little or no prenatal care are at highest risk of preterm birth.
- Eat right. Good nutrition during pregnancy makes for a stronger, healthier baby.
- Avoid alcohol and drugs. Exposure to these harmful substances during pregnancy decreases the oxygen supply to developing tissues. This can harm the part of the baby's brain that regulates breathing. The risk of SIDS increases eightfold in infants of substance-abusing mothers. Researchers believe that drugs such as opiates and cocaine constrict blood vessels in the placenta, reducing oxygen supply to the preborn baby. As a result, a baby's cardiorespiratory control centers may develop abnormally and are more likely to fail.

Another Great Reason to Breastfeed

Breastfeeding has long been cited as an important factor in a baby's overall health and development. Studies show a lower incidence of SIDS in breastfed babies. Here are possible reasons why:

- Breast milk enhances neurological development, helping the respiratory control center of the brain develop.
- Nutrients in breast milk fight infections that may harm a baby's respiratory health.

- Breastfeeding reduces gastroesophageal reflux (see page 23), which can cause stop-breathing episodes.
- Breastfed babies are more easily aroused from sleep.
- Breastfeeding improves a baby's breathing and swallowing coordination.
- Nursing stimulates the maternal hormones that increase a mother's awareness of her baby.

No Smoking, Please!

Studies show that exposure to cigarette smoke at least doubles the risk of SIDS, and heavy maternal smoking—more than twenty cigarettes a day—increases the risk fivefold.

Even passive smoking can increase the risk of SIDS. Suppose you were about to take your baby into a room when you noticed the following sign posted on the door:

WARNING!
THIS ROOM CONTAINS POISONOUS GASES THAT ARE LINKED TO CANCER AND LUNG DAMAGE. THEY ARE ESPECIALLY HARMFUL TO THE BREATHING PASSAGES OF YOUNG INFANTS.

You certainly wouldn't take your baby into that room! But that is exactly what you expose your baby to when he spends time in a room frequented by smokers.

Smoking interferes with the development of the cardiorespiratory control centers in a baby's brain. In addition, smoke paralyzes the cilia (tiny filaments that clear mucus from the air passages), compromising baby's breathing. In addition, mothers who smoke have lower levels of prolactin, the hormone that regulates milk production. Prolactin deficiency may lead to diminished maternal awareness of and responsiveness to an infant's needs.

Sleep Safely

The sleeping environment you provide for your infant also plays a significant role in reducing the risk of SIDS. Here are some sleep safety tips:

- Put baby to sleep on her back rather than her tummy. Babies' arousability from sleep (an infant's built-in protective mechanism) is greater when they sleep on their backs. Studies show that back-sleeping has decreased the risk of SIDS by as much as 30 to 50 percent in some countries, including the United States. A baby sleeping facedown may press her head into the mattress, forming a pocket of air around her face. As a result, she rebreathes exhaled air that has diminished oxygen.
- Avoid putting baby to sleep on unsafe surfaces, such as beanbag chairs or couches.
- Don't sleep with your baby while you are under the influence of any substance that diminishes your sensitivity to your baby's presence.
- Avoid overheating your baby during sleep.

Whether or not sleep-sharing lowers a baby's risk of SIDS is a controversial issue, but we believe that safe co-sleeping is a powerful SIDS risk-reduction factor. Current research suggests that SIDS may be a defect in a baby's normal arousability from sleep, so it's common sense that any sleeping arrangement that increases baby's arousability and mother's awareness would lower the risk of SIDS. This is exactly what sleep-sharing does.

The good news is that SIDS is no longer considered a mysterious cloud that hangs over a baby's crib waiting to snatch her last breath. While there is no guaranteed protection against Sudden Infant Death Syndrome, taking these preventive measures can reduce your risk and worry of losing a baby to SIDS.

Tummy Sleepers and SIDS

Q   *I have a four-month-old who was sleeping on her back just fine. But now that she can turn over, she often flips over onto her tummy as soon as I put her down to sleep. I know that sleeping on her back is important for reducing the risk of SIDS. What should I do?*

A   Placing an infant to sleep on her back has been shown to lower the baby's risk of SIDS (Sudden Infant Death Syndrome). In countries with Back to Sleep campaigns advising parents to place their infants on their backs at bedtime, SIDS rates have fallen 30 to 50 percent.

Remember, however, that this is a statistical correlation only. It does not mean that if your baby sleeps on her tummy, she is going to die of SIDS. Current SIDS rates are around one in a thousand babies, meaning that there is a 99.9 percent chance your child will remain healthy despite her sleep position. In fact, many SIDS researchers believe that a baby will naturally assume the sleep position that allows her to breathe most comfortably during the night.

While the cause of SIDS is still unknown, there is strong evidence that it may result when an at-risk baby has an immature breathing-regulating system that periodically shuts down in deep sleep. SIDS results if the system fails to restart the breathing process when the baby is in a deep sleep.

If your baby habitually flips over to sleep on her tummy after you put her down to sleep on her back, this may be the right sleeping position for her. If you want to be completely safe (or want to rest easily yourself), you might try putting your baby to sleep on her back and staying with her until she falls asleep. If she flips onto her tummy, turn her back over onto her back when she is in a deep sleep.

❦

The Benefits of Sleep-Sharing

Q *Every night my baby goes to bed at 8:30 and wakes up crying four hours later. I bring her into bed with me, but I have been reading a book that recommends letting babies cry themselves back to sleep. Is it something I should try? My parents strongly disagree with this theory, but I am really desperate.*

A The "let baby cry it out" advice has been around for a hundred years. However, listen to your parents on this subject, for they are right. Restraining yourself from responding to your baby is biologically incorrect. When your daughter cries, the blood flow to your breasts increases, and you experience a hormonal urge to pick her up and comfort her. Mothers are made that way. When you go against your instinct, you desensitize yourself to your own intuition and natural reflexes.

A baby's cry promotes the survival of the infant and the sensitivity of the mother. Letting your daughter cry it out is a lose-lose situation: Your baby loses trust in the signal value of her cry, and you lose faith in your ability to read and respond to her cry signals. Only a parent knows when and how long to let baby cry.

If you take your baby into your bed, you are responding in a healthy way. In fact, wherever both of you get the best night's sleep is the best arrangement for your family. We suggest that you start the night with her sleeping next to you so that she doesn't have to wake up and cry to demand her preferred sleeping arrangement. Sleeping next to you is likely to instill a healthy attitude toward sleep. If you give your daughter a secure nighttime parenting arrangement now, you will all sleep better eventually.

A brief history of how our own nighttime parenting practices evolved will show you why we believe this is the best style of nighttime parenting for most families.

Our first three babies were easy sleepers. We felt no need or desire to have them share our bed. Besides, I was a new member of the medical profession, whose party line was that sleeping with babies was weird and even dangerous. And at that time, all of the baby books preached the same old tired theme: Don't take your baby into your bed!

Then along came our fourth child, Hayden, born in 1978, whose birth changed our lives and our attitudes about sleep. Hayden hated her crib. Finally, one night, out of sheer exhaustion, rather than dutifully returning Hayden to her crib, Martha nestled Hayden next to her in our bed. She said, "I don't care what the books say! I'm tired, and I need some sleep!" Initially we had to get over those warnings about manipulation and terminal nighttime dependency. You are probably familiar with the long litany of "you'll be sorry" reasons. Well, we are not sorry. We are happy that Hayden opened up a whole wonderful nighttime world for us that we now can share with you.

At first we thought we were doing something unusual, but we soon discovered that many parents sleep with their babies. They just don't tell their doctors or their in-laws about it. In social settings, whenever the subject of sleep came up, we admitted that we slept with our babies. Other parents began to secretly "confess" that they did, too.

Most parents throughout the world sleep with their infants. Why is this beautiful custom taboo in our society? How could a culture be so educated in some things and so misguided in its parenting styles?

Though "bed-sharing" is the term frequently used in medical writing to describe the practice of sleeping with a baby, I prefer the term "sleep-sharing" because, as you will learn below, a baby shares more than just bed space. An infant and mother sleeping side by side share a great deal of interaction that is safe and healthy.

Sharing sleep is a mind-set, one in which parents are flexible enough to shift nighttime parenting styles as circumstances change. Every family goes through nocturnal juggling acts at different stages of a child's development. Sharing sleep reflects an attitude of acceptance of your baby as a little person with big needs. Your infant trusts that you, his parents, will be as available during the night as you are during the day.

Sharing sleep in our culture requires that you trust your intuition about parenting your baby instead of blindly accepting the norms of American society. By accepting and respecting your baby's needs when you welcome him into your bed, you are not spoiling your baby or letting him manipulate you.

Sleeping with Hayden opened our hearts and minds to the fact that there are many nighttime parenting styles, and parents need to be sensible and use whatever allows all family members to get the best sleep. Over the next sixteen years we slept with five of our babies (one at a time). Although having the bed to ourselves now is enjoyable, we still reflect on the special nighttime memories from our parenting past.

✍

Sleep-Sharing Gives Security

Q *My husband is stationed overseas for six months, and I've slept with my baby alone since she was born. I feel like this gives her an extra sense of security, especially with her father gone. Is this okay?*

A Our son James, an avid sailor, describes the sensitivity a sailor develops to his boat this way: "People often ask me how a sailor gets any sleep when ocean-racing solo. While sleeping, the lone sailor puts the boat on autopilot. Because the sailor is so in tune with his boat, if the wind shifts so that something is not quite right with the boat, the sailor wakes up." In the early years of sleeping with our babies, I observed a similar phenomenon, of the mother being in perfect harmony with her infant. I felt a special connection occurred between the sleep-sharing pair that had to be good for baby. Was it brain waves, motion, or something intangible that occurred between these two people during nighttime touch?

I remember awakening in the morning and gazing upon the contented face of our nine-month-old "sleeping beauty." I could tell when she was ascending from her level of deep sleep to light sleep. As she passed through the vulnerable period of awakening, she often reached out for her mother or me. When she touched one of us, an "I'm okay" expression would radiate from her face. Her eyes remained closed, and she did not awaken. However, she often awakened if she reached out and one of us was not within touching distance.

In our home, Martha and baby slept on their sides facing each other. Even if they started at a distance, baby would naturally gravitate toward Martha, their heads facing each other, a breath away. Many sleep-sharing mothers whom I have interviewed report that they spend most of their night sleeping on their backs or sides (as do their babies). These are positions that give mother and baby easier access to each other for breastfeeding. Observers of sleeping pairs also report the prevalence of the face-to-face position during sleep-sharing.

When I noticed this face-to-face, nose-to-nose position, I wondered if the exhalation from mother's nose might affect baby's breathing. Perhaps the face-to-face position allows mother's breath to stimulate baby's skin and therefore her breathing—a sort of "magic breath"—as they inhale and exhale.

Could there be sensors in a baby's nose that detect mother's breath, so that she is acting like a pacemaker or breathing stimulus? Researchers have in fact discovered that the lining of the nose is rich in receptors that may affect breathing, though their exact function is unknown. Perhaps some of these receptors are stimulated by mother's breath and/or smell, and thus affect baby's breathing. Exhaled breath is largely carbon dioxide, which acts as a respiratory stimulant. Recently researchers measured the exhaled air coming from the mother's nose while she was sleeping with her baby. They confirmed the logical suspicion that the closer mother's nose is, the higher the carbon dioxide concentration of her exhaled air; the concentration of carbon dioxide between the face-to-face pair is possibly just right to stimulate breathing.

As I watched the sleeping pair, the harmony in their breathing intrigued me. When Martha took a deep breath, baby took a deep breath. Martha would often enter a light sleep a few seconds before our babies did. They would gravitate toward one another. Then Martha, by some internal sensor, would turn toward baby and nurse or touch her. The pair would drift back to sleep, often without awakening. Also, there seemed to be occasional nearly simultaneous arousals, when either Martha or the baby would stir, and the other would move.

After spending hours watching, I was certain that each member of the sleep-sharing pair affected the sleep of the other but could only speculate about how this happened. Perhaps the mutual arousals allow mother and baby to "practice" waking up in response to a life-threatening event. If SIDS is a defect in arousability from sleep, perhaps this practice helps baby's arousability mature.

I was amazed by how much interaction went on between Martha and our babies when they shared sleep. Sometimes the baby would extend an arm, touch Martha, take a deep breath, and resettle. Martha would periodically semi-awaken to check on the baby, rearrange the covers, and then drift easily back to sleep. Keeping a baby appropriately covered for the right nighttime temperatures is a proven SIDS risk-lowering factor. This and other nighttime checks on baby's well-being are easier while sharing sleep. It seems that when baby and mother sleep together, they spend a great deal of time during the night checking on the presence of each other.

✍

Sleep-Sharing to Reduce the Risk of SIDS

Q *I've heard that sleeping with my baby may reduce the chance of SIDS. Is this true?*

A Yes, I believe it is true. The effect of sleeping arrangements on SIDS is, admittedly, a controversial and hotly debated issue mired in emotions and politics that often cloud both science and common sense. Consider the following evidence, then you be the judge.

SIDS was originally called crib death, and it is a fact that many more babies die alone from apparent SIDS than while sleeping in their parents' bed. The incidence of SIDS is lowest among populations that traditionally share sleep, with their SIDS rate increasing as their cultural environment changes. For example, SIDS rates are lowest in Asian countries, where parents and babies traditionally share sleep. In Hong Kong, where sleep-sharing is the norm, the

SIDS rate is around one-thirtieth that of the United States; in Japan, where sleep-sharing is also the norm, the SIDS rate is one-tenth that of the United States. However, according to a California study, the longer Asian immigrants live in the United States, the higher their rate of SIDS. This could be related to their adoption of a more detached nighttime parenting style.

More than twenty years ago, I formed the hypothesis that sleep-sharing lowered the risk of SIDS. In 1985 I wrote in my book *Nighttime Parenting,* "In those infants at risk for SIDS, natural mothering (unrestricted breast-feeding and sharing sleep with baby) will lower the risk of SIDS." As you will read below, new research is beginning to validate this hypothesis.

Scientific Studies on Sleep-Sharing

Q *Is there any scientific research that substantiates the health benefits of sleep-sharing? What made you feel confident that this was best for your babies as you practiced nighttime parenting?*

A In 1992, a new baby, Lauren, entered the Sears bedroom laboratory. This blessing, plus the availability of the new computer-assisted microtechnology, gave us the opportunity to finally study the effects of sleep-sharing on a baby's breathing in a natural home environment. Because this was the first time anyone had studied sleep-sharing in a nonlaboratory setting, we were invited to present the results of our study at the International Apnea Conference in 1993.

We set up equipment in our bedroom to study eight-week-old Lauren's breathing while she slept in two different arrangements. One night Lauren and Martha slept together in the same bed, as they were used to doing. The next night, Lauren slept alone in our bed, and Martha slept in an adjacent room. Lauren was wired to an electrocardiograph (which provided an electrical recording of her heart) and a computer that recorded her breathing movements, the airflow from her nose, and her blood oxygen.

The instrumentation was painless and didn't appear to disturb Lauren's sleep. The equipment was designed to detect only Lauren's physiological changes during sleep; it did not pick up Martha's signals. Martha nursed Lauren down to sleep in both arrangements and sensitively responded to Lauren's nighttime needs. A technician and I observed and recorded the information. The data were analyzed by computer and interpreted by a pediatric pulmonologist who was "blind" to the situation—that is, he didn't know whether the data he was analyzing came from the shared-sleeping or the solo-sleeping arrangement.

Our study revealed that Lauren breathed better when

sleeping next to Martha than when sleeping alone. Her breathing and her heart rate were more regular during shared sleep, and there were fewer "dips," low points in respiration and blood oxygen from stop-breathing episodes. On the night Lauren slept with Martha, there were in fact no dips in her blood oxygen. However, on the night when she slept alone, there were 132 dips. The results were similar in a study of a second infant whose parents graciously allowed us into their bedroom. We studied Lauren and the other infant again at five months. As expected, the physiological differences between shared and solo sleep were less pronounced at age five months than at age two months.

Certainly these studies would not stand up to scientific scrutiny because of the small sample. It would be presumptuous to draw sweeping conclusions from studies on only two babies. We meant this to be a pilot study. But what we did learn was that, with the availability of new microtechnology and in-home, nonintrusive monitoring, my belief about the protective effects of sharing sleep was a testable hypothesis. I hoped this preliminary study would stimulate other SIDS researchers to scientifically study the physiological effects of sharing sleep in a natural home environment.

Current Research on Sleep-Sharing

Over the past few years, nearly a million dollars of government research money have been devoted to sleep-sharing research. At this writing, the physiological effects of sleep-sharing are finally being studied in sleep laboratories that are set up to mimic as much as possible the home bedroom. The infants in these studies have all ranged from two to five months in age. Here are the preliminary findings based on studies of mother-infant pairs in a sleep-sharing versus solitary-sleeping arrangement.

- The pairs showed more synchronous arousals when sharing sleep than when sleeping separately. When one member of the sleep-sharing pair stirred, coughed, or changed sleeping stages, the other member also changed, often without awakening.
- Each member of the sleep-sharing pair tended often, but not always, to be in the same stage of sleep for longer periods if they slept together.
- Sleep-sharing babies spent less time in each cycle of deep sleep. Sleep-sharing mothers didn't get less total deep sleep. This is welcome news to mothers who worry they will get less sleep if they share sleep.
- Sleep-sharing infants aroused more often and spent more time breastfeeding than did solitary sleepers. Yet in studies done by Dr. McKenna and Dr. Mosko at the University of California, the sleep-sharing mothers did not report awakening more frequently.
- Sleep-sharing infants tended to sleep more often on their backs or sides and less often on their tummies, a factor that itself could lower the SIDS risk.
- Sleep-sharers experienced frequent interaction and mutual touch. What one did affected the nighttime behavior of the other.

Sleep-sharing research is in its infancy, and the results of these studies are too preliminary to draw definite conclusions on SIDS risk reduction. But it seems evident that shared-sleepers do sleep differently from solo sleepers. Whether or not this difference is protective remains to be proven. I believe it is. It is likely that within a few years scientists will confirm what insightful mothers have long known: Something good and healthful occurs when mothers and babies share sleep.

✍

Sleeping on Mom or Dad

Q *My baby likes to fall asleep on my chest at night. But after I put him down at my side, he wakes up crying until I put him back on my chest. I can't sleep this way. Help!*

A Many kids ago we learned a helpful survival tactic: Babies do what they do because they're designed that way. When we were confused about a certain behavior, we got behind the eyes of our children and tried to imagine things from their viewpoint. Picture yourself as your baby, lying on your parent's chest (a high-touch arrangement that we call the "warm fuzzy" for Dad and the "warm smoothie" for Mom). Baby is inches away from the soothing rhythm of your heartbeat that he grew accustomed to in Mom's womb. The rhythmic rise and fall of your chest during breathing is another high-touch soother. Likewise, the warm feel of your skin and the warm air from your nose brushing his scalp comforts him. Add more sleep-inducing touches by Mom or Dad, such as the "neck nestle" on page 52, and you can imagine that baby thinking, "Ah, life is good!" It is no wonder that babies prefer sleeping on a warm, moving body rather than behind bars in a crib.

While some babies are born sleepers, for others sleeping alone is scary; it's as if they need the touch from a person to help them adjust to life outside the womb. Soon, as baby's sleep habits mature, he will be able to sleep at an increasing distance from you.

In the meantime, try the following:

- When your baby seems ready for sleep, wear him around in a sling until he is fully asleep and then ease him into his bed (see "wearing down" on page 52).
- Continue the physical touch, yet in a different way: rock, sing, or nurse him off to sleep.
- Make a medley of lullabies that are proven sleep-inducers, and try mothering or fathering your baby to sleep to the sounds of these familiar lullabies. Leave the music on when you lay him down.
- Try a "moving bed." When it is time for baby to go to sleep (or you are ready for baby to go to sleep), put your baby safely in a car seat and drive until your baby is fully asleep.
- Take advantage of "mechanical mothers," such as rocking your baby in a cradle or using a motor-oscillating bassinet or mechanical swing. Though we generally dis-

courage mechanical nurturing substitutes, occasionally these parenting props can pinch-hit when the real parent is exhausted.

If the above techniques are not working, regard this high-touch nighttime parenting style as an all-too-quickly passing stage. Take it as a compliment that your baby prefers your warm body to some personless prop.

Using a Car Seat as a Substitute Crib

Q *My baby cannot relax unless she is in her car seat. Is this a safe place for her to fall asleep?*

A Letting baby fall asleep in a car seat is safe provided the baby's caregivers take certain precautions. Since babies up to 20 pounds must always ride in a rear-facing safety seat in the back seat, an adult should ride in the back seat with the baby. Frequently check on the breathing of the sleeping baby, especially during a long drive. Some infants experience stop-breathing episodes during a long ride in a car seat. This may be due to the slumped position, which causes baby's abdomen to be pushed up against the chest, compromising breathing. Another possible factor is that the stomach outlet may be pushed higher than the inlet, causing gastroesophageal reflux (see page 23) and consequent stop-breathing episodes. To tilt the car seat back slightly, you can place a tightly rolled bath towel under the front edge of the seat. Newer car seats allow babies to be positioned in a less bent reclining position.

Never put the car-seated baby with you in the front seat. If you're alone and need to check on baby or attend to her, pull over and stop the car.

These car-seat precautions are especially important for premature babies and infants who have exhibited breathing problems. Falling asleep in a car seat gets progressively safer as baby gets older, when it becomes a time-tested technique for settling the reluctant sleeper.

◈

Falling Asleep Beside
Mom or Dad

Q *I let my two-month-old fall asleep with me on my bed and then transfer him to his crib. Am I setting up a bad habit?*

A Congratulations! You are promoting good sleep habits. The purpose of nighttime parenting is to instill a healthy sleep attitude in your baby. This lets baby know that sleep is a pleasant state to be entered without fear. Falling asleep next to Mommy or Daddy is a wonderful way to do just that. If your baby had his way, he would naturally choose to sleep snuggled against his favorite person in the whole world instead of alone and isolated behind the bars of his crib. This bedtime style is especially helpful for busy babies who find it difficult to wind down after a long day of growing and exploring.

You may be worried that if you continue to let your child drift off to sleep in your bed, he will never learn to sleep on his own. This common concern comes out of the sleep association theory, which supposes that if baby learns to associate falling asleep with his parents' bed, he'll grow to depend on that environment. Consequently, when baby wakes up in the middle of the night, he will not be able to go back to sleep on his own and will demand to be taken back to his parents' bedroom.

While there is some merit to the sleep association theory, we prefer to think of it this way: Nighttime parenting is a long-term investment. Babies need something or someone to attach to when they sleep, something comforting to help them make the transition from a state of wakefulness to a sleeping state. While an older baby may soothe himself to sleep with a variety of props, such as a stuffed animal or his blankie, wouldn't it be better for him to bond with you? When you think of association in this way, you can see the payoff on your long-term investment: a child who is confident that his parents will always watch over him, day or night, and who has learned to value people over things.

As long as your nighttime routine works for you and your child, please continue what you are doing. He'll enjoy cuddling his way to sleep with you. The time he spends in his crib will allow him to grow more accustomed to sleeping in his own space. When he gets to be a little older, he'll eventually learn to go to sleep on his own in his crib or in his toddler bed. But more than likely he'll still want you to participate in his bedtime ritual. Whether you use bedtime stories, lullabies, gentle rocking, or a combination of techniques, young children need to be parented to sleep.

❦

Transitioning Techniques
Help Newborns Relax

Q *Our three-month-old son thrives on being awake and active—during the day and at night. When it is time for bed, I have to hold him close to me and rock him until he finally gives in and falls asleep. How can I teach him to slowly unwind at bedtime?*

A Many infants need help making the transition from being awake to falling asleep. This should be a function of your bedtime routine. The effectiveness of transitioning techniques can vary depending on the stage of your baby's development. What works one week may not work the next. Here are some techniques that may help:

- *Nursing down.* Nestle next to your baby and breastfeed or bottlefeed him to sleep. Feeding baby to sleep works especially well after a bath and massage. The continuum from warm bath to warm arms to warm breast (or warm milk) to warm bed is a powerful recipe for baby's sleep.
- *Rocking or walking down.* Rocking baby to sleep in a bedside rocking chair or slider helps him relax and realize it is bedtime. Or try walking with him while patting his back and singing lullabies. The monotonous motion will gently bore him to sleep.
- *Fathering down.* Encourage Dad to try the "neck

nestle." Rest baby's head against the front of your neck with your chin over the top of his head and rock him to sleep. The vibration of the deeper male voice should lull baby to sleep. If he won't drift off to sleep while you rock him, lie down next to him (still in the neck nestle position) and let him fall asleep draped over your chest (the "warm fuzzy" technique). Once your baby is in a deep sleep, ease him into his bed and tiptoe away.

- *Wearing down.* Some babies get so revved up during the day that they have trouble winding down at night. To help your baby relax, wear him in a sling for about a half hour before the designated bedtime. When he is sleeping soundly, ease him out of the sling into his bed. If your baby is used to being nursed to sleep, let Dad try wearing the baby down in this manner to give Mom a break.

- *Nestling down.* Some babies demand more effort than others. Your infant may just not want to go to sleep on his own. After you rock or feed your baby, lie down with him next to you and nestle in close until he is sound asleep. We call this the "teddy-bear snuggle."

Try a Bed on Wheels

If you've tried all of the above and baby still resists falling asleep, try strapping him into his car seat and driving around until he falls asleep. After he falls asleep, carry the car seat and baby inside and leave him strapped in until his first night waking. If he drifts off into a deep sleep—open palms, arms dangling loosely at his side, facial muscles completely still—you can probably ease him out of the car seat and into his own bed without waking him. See page 54 for tips on getting your baby to sleep longer.

❦

Growth Spurts and Night Waking

Q *I think my baby is having a growth spurt because she wants to eat all the time. She also is not sleeping as soundly at night and waking easily. Is there a correlation?*

A If you look at infant growth charts, you would think that infants grow in a smooth, steady progression. But most babies grow in bursts and pauses. The hormones responsible for growth are secreted more at night. Some babies wake up more at night during growth spurts, since sudden hormonal changes can trigger a change in sleep habits. Also, since tiny children have tiny tummies, during growth spurts they often want—and need—an occasional night feeding. Growth spurts often signal that a change in nighttime parenting is required.

If she is awakening frequently in her crib and experiences separation anxiety, sleeping closer to you may lessen the frequent night waking. Also, tank her up with more frequent feedings throughout the day, plus just before bed. Once these growth spurts of early childhood lessen in frequency and intensity, she will literally grow out of her frequent night waking.

$$\mathcal{E}$$

Stay-Asleep Techniques

Q *We have no problem getting our eight-week-old baby to sleep. But any noise, light, or physical discomfort is her wake-up call to start crying. I spend half the night calming her down, trying to get her to relax. What am I doing wrong?*

A As anyone who has cared for a baby will tell you, getting a baby to sleep is only half the battle. The bigger challenge is getting her to stay asleep. This means you must create that optimal bedtime condition in which your baby is most likely to go back to sleep on her own when she awakens during the night. Here are some ways to do just that:

• *Dress her for the occasion.* In the early months, many babies like to "sleep tight," securely swaddled in a cotton baby blanket. Older infants prefer to "sleep loose" and will often sleep for longer stretches if they have more freedom of movement. Sometimes you can condition baby to associate swaddling with sleep by dressing her loosely during the day but more tightly at night. (For more information on the best sleepwear for baby, turn to page 13.)

- *Keep her bedroom quiet.* Most babies don't need absolute quiet to sleep, but sudden noises awaken some babies easily. For these more sensitive babies, oil the joints and springs of a squeaky crib, put the dog outside if he barks, turn off the ringer if there is a phone nearby, and make any other adjustments to her sleep environment that you can. (For more information on noise and infant sleep, see page 16.)
- *Block bedroom light.* Hang opaque shades in the bedroom to block out the morning sun. This might buy you an extra hour of sleep if you have one of those little roosters who awaken with the first ray of sunlight.
- *Import sleepy-time sounds.* The steady noise produced by fans, air conditioners, and vacuum cleaners has been proven to be an effective baby lullaby. Also helpful are a bubbling fish tank filter, a ticking clock, a metronome set at sixty beats a minute, or a tape recording of any of these sounds. Some musical selections also make good sleepy-time sound tracks. (See page 73 for the best music for infant sleep.)
- *Leave behind a little bit of Mom.* If you have a clingy baby who doesn't like to be separated from you, leave a breast pad in her cradle or play a continuous tape recording of yourself singing a lullaby.

Common Causes of Frequent Nighttime Waking

Q *My three-month-old constantly wakes up during the night, and I often can't figure out what she wants. I usually just try to hold her and give her a bottle. What should I do?*

A While babies do sleep more lightly and for shorter periods than adults, they need their rest as much as adults do. Babies won't awaken frequently unless there's a reason. Consider these possibilities:

- *Nighttime separation anxiety.* Your baby may want to sleep closer to you. Try some different sleeping arrangements until you find one that lets everyone get a good night's sleep. Your baby may sleep best snuggled safely next to you in your bed or in a bassinet or co-sleeper next to your bed (see page 12). Babies' nighttime needs often change as they reach a new stage of development, so even if she used to sleep well in the next room, you may find that some experimentation is in order. A sleeping arrangement that worked in the past may not be appropriate today. If you are not comfortable with your baby sleeping in your room or in your bed, you can gradually move her sleep space farther from you as she gets older and sleeps for longer periods in deeper stages of sleep.

- *Gastroesophageal reflux*. GER, as explained on page 23, is the most common hidden medical cause of night waking. GER can be successfully treated with medication, so discuss the possibility with your pediatrician.
- *Allergies*. If your baby is particularly fussy after her feedings, she may be allergic to her formula. If you are breastfeeding, she may be allergic to a food in your diet (dairy is a common culprit). Symptoms of formula or food allergy include a red, sandpaper-like rash on her cheeks or a red, raised rash around her anus. If you suspect food allergies are at the root of your baby's sleepless nights, try changing formulas or, with the advice of a doctor or nutritionist, eliminating common "fussy foods" from your diet if you're breastfeeding. She may also have an allergy to dust mites in the bedroom, a pet, or stuffed toys on her shelf. Talk with your doctor for answers.

ℰℬ

Responding to Frequent Nighttime Waking

Q *Should our six-month-old breastfed baby be sleeping through the night? Recently the period between wakings has decreased. Should we respond to every sound he makes at night, or should we let him try to get back to sleep on his own?*

A The most oft-repeated remedy to night waking is the tired, old advice to let baby cry it out. This is easy for others to say, since they are not biologically wired to your baby. The simple fact is that when your baby cries, the blood flow to your breasts increases and you have a biological urge to respond.

Between six and nine months, many infants who were previously sleeping for longer stretches begin waking more often. This may happen for two reasons:

1. Pain associated with teething.
2. Separation anxiety, especially at night, which may intensify at this age.

Studies have also shown that breastfed babies awaken more frequently for night feedings than bottlefed babies do. Nighttime nursing is a highly pleasurable experience for a baby. Because Mom isn't busy or preoccupied, he can nestle next to her and truly enjoy the feeding.

The key to nighttime parenting is to balance your baby's need for comfort and security with your need for sleep. After all, a family with a thriving, secure baby and sleep-deprived parents is out of balance.

If your baby starts to wake more frequently, consider the following nighttime parenting tips:

- *Play each cry by ear.* Only you will know when to respond quickly to your infant's cry and when you can let him try to resettle himself. Your response time can lengthen as baby grows. In other words, you don't have to respond to a six-month-old baby as quickly as to a six-day-old infant. Also, there are times when your need to sleep is greater than baby's desire to nurse.
- *Let Dad take turns responding to baby's nighttime needs.* When the baby wakes up, encourage Dad to rock and comfort him. This will teach your little one that nighttime is for sleeping rather than feeding.
- *Tank up your baby with extra feedings during the day and awaken him for a full feeding before you go to bed.* Six- to nine-month-olds often get so busy during the day perfecting their sitting and crawling skills that they forget to eat. As a result, they try to make up for missed feedings at night. An evening feeding of rice cereal and bananas may help your little one sleep for longer stretches.
- *Try different sleeping arrangements*—from sleeping next to you to sleeping in a crib in his own room—until you find one that gives all family members the best night's sleep.

☙

The Advantages of
Sleep-Sharing for Moms

Q *I'm expecting a baby next month, and I'm consid-
ering sleep-sharing. I've read about the benefits for
babies, but are there any advantages for moms, too?*

A Yes! Not only do babies sleep more soundly in the
family bed, but most parents—especially moms—do, too.
Here are some of the reasons:

- *Sleep-sharing prevents separation anxiety.* Baby is not
  the only one who is separation-sensitive at night. A new
  mother also experiences anxiety when her baby is not
  nearby. She lies awake and wonders, "Is my baby all
  right?" The farther away she is from baby, the deeper the
  anxiety.
- *Sleep-sharing allows Mom to maintain harmony with
  her baby.* Achieving harmony with your baby during the
  day is an important part of attachment parenting.
  Sharing sleep allows this harmony to continue.

  Physical closeness causes mothers and babies to share
  sleep cycles; their internal clocks are synchronized.
  When baby wakes during a vulnerable period, mother is
  likely to be in light sleep. She can help baby settle again
  without her own sleep cycles being seriously disturbed.
  It may take a little while to master sleep harmony, but

mothers who have achieved this synchronization report that they feel rested. Mothers must first learn to sleep like babies to help their babies learn to sleep like adults.

When babies and mothers sleep separately, their sleep cycles are not in harmony. Baby may awaken during his light sleep state, but mother may still be in her deep sleep state. Being awakened from a state of deep sleep to tend to baby is what makes nighttime parenting unattractive and leads to sleep-deprived mothers and fathers. When sleep harmony is not achieved, nighttime parenting becomes a duty rather than a natural nurturing experience.

- *Sleep-sharing lets Mom resettle more quickly after waking.* Picture a typical solo-sleeping scenario. Baby wakes up alone behind bars, out of touch. Baby cries and no one is there, so his cries become louder. Because separation anxiety sets in, his cries escalate further and eventually wake up even the most distant mother. Then Mom jumps up and staggers down the hall to baby's room, and by the time she gets to baby he is wide awake and upset. Likewise, Mom is wide awake and upset. A crying, angry baby takes longer to settle than a baby who is comforted before he is totally awake. When baby is finally settled, Mom is wide awake and too upset to resettle easily.

- *Breastfeeding is easier.* When mother's and baby's sleep cycles are in harmony, night nursing is less tiring. Mothers usually find it much easier to roll over and nurse than to get out of bed, go into another room, turn on a light, pick up a crying baby, settle in a rocking chair, and finally feed the baby. By this time both mother and baby are wide awake. Family-bed nursing meets the needs of the nursing couple without either one becoming fully awake.

Many mothers have told me that when they sleep with their babies, their sleep lightens and they almost wake up about thirty seconds before their babies awaken for a feeding. By being able to anticipate the feeding, mothers usually start nursing just as the baby begins to squirm and reach for the nipple. The babies do not fully awaken and drift back into deep sleep right after nursing.

- *Sleep-sharing is contemporary.* Sleeping with their babies fits in with the busy lifestyles of moms today. As ever more parents are separated from their babies during the day, sleeping together allows babies and parents to reconnect at night to make up for missed touch time during the day. Sleep-sharing is particularly valuable for a working mother, especially if she wishes to continue breastfeeding. Besides allowing baby and mother to reconnect, breastfeeding at night helps keep mother's milk supply up, so that she can continue to breastfeed even if she is working full-time or part-time outside the home. As an added benefit, the hormones stimulated by night nursing relax a working mother, helping her unwind from a busy day's work and get a better night's sleep.

The Long-Term Effects of
Sharing Sleep

Q *Is sleeping with my baby going to help him become a brighter and happier child?*

A   There are many variables that contribute to a child's growth and development. However, psychologists agree that the quantity and quality of mothering does affect the emotional and intellectual development of the child. Extending the practice of daytime attachment parenting into nighttime parenting does have long-term effects on the child.

One of these effects is in the area of intimacy. Many psychologists and marriage counselors report that one common problem of contemporary teenagers and adults is that they have difficulty forming a genuinely close and intimate relationship with another person. Sharing sleep teaches a child to be comfortable being in touch with somebody; it doesn't substitute things for people. A child-hood need for intimacy that is unfulfilled never completely goes away. Psychologists report that many adult fears and sleep problems can be traced back to sleep disturbances during childhood.

Sleep-sharing creates pleasant memories. One of the most precious gifts you can give your child is a vivid memory of happy childhood attachments, such as being parented to sleep in the arms of his father or mother. I remember looking over at the baby sleeping next to me and seeing a contented look on her face that said, "Thanks, Mom and Dad, for having me here." And I'll never forget how happy our children were when they awoke in our bed. Those memories will last a lifetime.

Mom Can't Sleep with Baby There

Q *I want to sleep with my three-month-old baby because I have read so much about the benefits of sleep-sharing. Yet when he snuggles next to me, I don't seem to sleep as well. So I've been putting him down in his crib. Any suggestions?*

A This is a common complaint among parents who didn't share sleep starting at the baby's birth. By three months it may take a bit longer to get used to this arrangement. Still, the benefits are definitely worth the effort— and after a couple of weeks, you will probably be able to sleep through more of your baby's gurgles and swats.

One way to overcome your restless nights is to experiment with the sleeping distance between you and your baby. For each mother and child, there may be a distance that is most conducive to sleep. Too much or too little distance between an infant and his mother can cause one or both of them to awaken more frequently during the night. When babies wake up, they often want to reach out and feel for their mother's presence before drifting back to sleep, and if they're too far away they can't do that. Some moms, on the other hand, say that when baby sleeps too close, they startle at their child's every noise and movement.

If your problems sleeping with your baby continue, try using a co-sleeper (see page 12). This works well for many mothers, especially those who are light sleepers but still want to enjoy the intimacy of sleep-sharing.

Finding Your Own Nighttime Parenting Style

Q *We adore our baby, but we really don't want to do this "co-sleeping" thing. Is there something wrong with us?*

A   There is no one right place for an infant to sleep. Where all family members get the best night's sleep is the right arrangement for your family. Parents choose to co-sleep with their infants for different reasons. Some find it more convenient, especially for frequent night nursing. Other parents choose to sleep with their babies because they don't have enough daytime touch with their infants, so sleeping with their baby allows them to reconnect at night. Some infants and parents do not sleep as soundly when sleeping close to each other, and some parents do not sleep as well with babies in their bed. Like all aspects of parenting, your chosen style of nighttime parenting needs to be one that you personally enjoy; otherwise, it won't work, and your infant will sense this. Certainly, you are not less of a parent if you don't want to sleep with your baby. A very caring and sensitive mother of five in our practice once told us, "Quite honestly, I don't want our baby in our bed. We have four other children and by the time evening comes, I've had enough of kids and want some time alone with my husband."

You are not being a neglectful mother if you don't sleep with your baby. You are a wise mother to have a realistic appraisal of your nighttime needs. Just as a breastfeeding mother is not a better mother than a mother who bottle-feeds, a mother who shares sleep with her baby is not better than one who doesn't. Don't feel pressured into a nighttime parenting style that you don't want to do, simply because you read about it or your friends endorse it. You may have a baby who is not separation-sensitive and may sleep quite well in her crib at night. The key is to stay connected with your baby, and there are many styles of daytime parenting that can help you do this.

Thumb Sucking

Q *My baby must suck her thumb to fall asleep. I'm worried she is overly stressed. Do you think this could be the reason?*

A It's helpful for infants to develop their own night-time self-soothing techniques so that they don't always have to rely on parents to get them back to sleep when they awaken. This is the concept of sleep associations: The prop that your infant uses to go to sleep will be the same one that she expects when she awakens. And that's the beauty of the ever-present and always available nighttime thumb.

Infants are born with an insatiable desire to suck. Your preborn baby probably sucked her thumb even while in your womb. The reason that babies suck their thumbs so much at night is that sleep is thought to be a regressive state during which they return to innate reflexes, such as thumb sucking. When your baby wakes up, she probably automat-ically clicks into this sucking reflex and reaches for her thumb. The habit of thumb sucking off to sleep is certainly better than a bottle of milk or juice (which can cause cavi-ties) or a pacifier, which baby cannot locate at night.

Don't feel that she is sucking her thumb because she is tense or missing some parenting. Many infants just enjoy the comfort of their thumb and use it as a back-to-sleep prop in the middle of the night.

Thumb sucking can be a problem if it continues into toddlerhood, since the occasional child will put enough pressure on the upper front teeth to cause an overbite. If during your child's regular checkups your doctor mentions that she is developing an overbite, it's time to replace the thumb with a more tooth-friendly sleep prop, such as a large stuffed toy that she can put her arm around so she can't reach her thumb. The nighttime thumbsucking stage of early infancy usually passes once the teeth are large enough to be harmed by this habit.

Safe Sleep-Sharing with a GER Baby

Q *Our five-week-old son has been diagnosed with gastroesophageal reflux. He's been sleeping in our bed. Is there a way to safely continue doing this?*

A Attachment parenting, the high-touch caregiving style that includes sleep-sharing, is actually beneficial for GER (see page 23), so there is no need to give up sleep-sharing.

The dilemma with GER is that back-sleeping, which is

the recommended position for lowering the risk of SIDS, aggravates a baby's GER. As a compromise, place your son to sleep on his left side facing you. In this position, gravity will help keep the milk down because the gastric inlet will be higher than the outlet. But if your baby settles on his tummy only, don't worry. Although back-sleeping is preferred, the current recommendation is that babies with a medical condition that is improved by sleeping on their tummies should be placed to sleep on their tummies. GER, which can itself trigger stop-breathing episodes, is one of those conditions.

If your son has severe GER, try a reflux wedge (available at infant-product stores), which enables baby to sleep propped up at a 30-degree angle. If the wedge is difficult to use in your bed, try it in the Arm's Reach Co-Sleeper (see page 12).

⌘

The Attachment Approach to Nighttime Parenting

Q *My five-month-old won't sleep through the night. I tried the sleep-training method for weeks, but things just got worse. We've ruled out illness and tried white noise. We stick to the same bedtime routine every night. My baby also has a blankie and uses a pacifier. Although our child sleeps best in our bed, our pediatrician has advised against this. I am so sleep-deprived. Please help!*

A There are two schools of thought about getting babies to sleep. One is a rigid method of sleep training. This is where baby is awake when you put her down in a crib. She is left to cry herself to sleep so that she learns to "self-soothe" and doesn't develop sleep associations that require someone else to put her to sleep. The theory is that a baby who learns to put herself to sleep will be able to fall back to sleep on her own when she wakes up in the night. This method has been around since the 1890s and was popularized primarily by male university sleep-laboratory researchers, certainly not by mothers who have parented many children.

We do not subscribe to the sleep-training method. We believe it creates an unhealthy attitude about sleep, causing a baby to view sleep as a fearful state to enter and to remain in. You have tried this method without success and learned a valuable lesson in parenting: If something doesn't work for you, drop it—even if your pediatrician advises it. In fact, in our writings we recommend that you never ask your doctor the following three questions:

1. Where should my baby sleep?
2. How long should my baby nurse?
3. Should I let my baby cry?

In our view, these are parenting-style issues that are better answered by an experienced parent. And, let's not forget—you know your baby the best!

The style of nighttime parenting we advocate is called the "attachment approach." With this approach, rather than viewing sleep as a state you can force a baby into, you create an environment that allows sleep to overtake the baby. This method helps the baby develop a healthy attitude about sleep, which is what you have done by sleeping with your baby.

If you and your baby both sleep best together, that is the right arrangement for your family. There's no need to worry that your child will never leave your bed. She will. Just enjoy the present, and the future will take care of itself. The time spent in your bed is a very short period in the total life of your child. However, the memories of your love and availability will last her a lifetime.

✍

Fear of Rolling Over
on Baby

Q *I want to sleep with our new baby, but I am worried
I will roll over and smother her. Is this possible?*

A The good news is that overlying (rolling over on
baby) rarely happens. In fact, overlying has gotten an
unfair reputation. Each night all over the world millions of
parents sleep with their babies, and the babies wake up just
fine. There are many more crib accidents than sleep-
sharing accidents.

The same subconscious awareness of boundaries that
keeps you from rolling off the bed prevents you from
rolling onto your baby. Mothers who have been interviewed on the subject of sharing sleep claim to be so physically and mentally aware of their baby's presence even
while sleeping that they would be extremely unlikely to
roll over onto their babies. Even if they did, their babies
would be likely to put up such a fuss that the mothers
would awaken in an instant.

Martha, a ten-year veteran of sleep-sharing, believes
that because a breastfeeding mother usually has such full
breasts at night, she is unlikely to roll over onto her chest
without being awakened by pain. Also, breastfeeding
sleep-sharing mothers nearly always sleep facing their

infants, so they're unlikely to roll over onto their backs and smother their babies that way.

The bad news is that overlying does happen. Most cases of proven overlying (most of the suspected cases were not proven) have been the result of some atypical sleeping arrangement, such as:

- too small a bed
- too many people in a bed
- parents under the influence of drugs or alcohol
- an unsafe sleeping surface

If you enjoy sleeping with your baby and all of you are getting enough sleep in this arrangement, don't let the fear of overlying discourage you from feeling secure with this time-honored custom.

Naptime Cuddling

Q *My two-month-old has no problem sleeping alone in her bassinet at night, but the only way she will nap during the day is in my arms or on my lap. Am I setting up a bad habit by allowing this, and will she grow out of it?*

A You are not setting up a bad habit by letting your baby sleep in your arms or on your lap. In fact, you are creating a good habit.

Many kids ago we learned that babies are able to communicate their needs to their caregivers. It is up to their caregivers to learn how to listen. If your baby will nap only in your arms or on your lap during the day, yet she sleeps well alone at night, let the sleeping baby be. If you try to change her daytime sleeping habits, you may wind up with a night waker. Most parents can handle any snooze habits during the day if their baby sleeps well at night.

It is often difficult for parents to discern whether their baby is communicating a need or merely a preference. But after thirty years of parenting eight children, we've learned that it's best to consider any cue a baby gives during the first six months as a need and to respond accordingly. Don't worry that you may be spoiling your infant or that she is manipulating you. This type of thinking will only create a distance between you and your baby and lessen your natural ability to read and respond to her cues. Besides, most mothers of two-month-olds need daytime naps themselves. When our babies went through this in-arms stage, if Martha felt tired, she would simply lie down with the baby so that they could nap together. In this way, the baby's need was translated into a restful habit for Martha—a pleasure she would not have indulged if baby had not requested it.

Eventually your baby will outgrow her naptime cuddling need, and then you may long for the days when she wanted you to hold her more. Have you ever heard of a parent who looked back and wished she had held her baby less? We haven't. Most of us wish we had held our children more!

❧

Baby Bedtime Music

Q *How do I know what sounds will help my baby sleep and what will keep her awake? I've read that music may help babies sleep better. What kind of music is most effective?*

A One of the best acoustic infant sleep aids is white noise, a mixture of sound waves that extend over a wide frequency range. You can buy a white-noise generator at most department stores. Also effective are the monotonous, repetitive sounds of air conditioners, fans, dish-washers, and vacuum cleaners (depending on its volume, you could try running it in a closet). Even better is noise that closely resembles the sound of the womb, such as running water, a metronome set for sixty beats per minute, a ticking clock, a bubbling fish tank filter, or recordings of the ocean or actual womb sounds.

If you prefer music, choose pieces with steady, consistent rhythms. We suggest classical music with tempos that rise and fall slowly, like that of composers Ravel, Mozart, Vivaldi, Dvořák, Debussy, Bach, and Haydn. Try to find recordings that don't use a full orchestra. Solo cello and acoustic guitar performances are good bets. The jarring beats and sudden tempo changes that characterize rock music, on the other hand, are sure to keep baby wide awake (and may upset her quite a bit as well).

Experiment to find the best sounds for your baby's slumber. Then edit the best sounds together onto a tape to be played continuously in her bedroom.

ℒ

Transitions: To the Crib, Off the Breast

Q *My seven-month-old daughter has slept with us since she was one month old. Since I'm still breastfeeding, this arrangement works out well. Within the next month or two I plan to start weaning, but I'd like my baby to make the transition to her crib first. What is the best way to make this transition?*

A   Babies have a hard time making the transition from their parent's bed to their own. This is easy to understand if you consider it from your baby's viewpoint: For months, she has been used to sleeping first-class, nestled next to her favorite person in the world with her mouth only inches from her favorite gourmet food. Why would an infant willingly exchange such bliss for sleeping in a dark room alone behind bars? It's no wonder babies protest this downgrade!

We recommend sleep-sharing with unrestricted breast-feeding for as long as possible. However, if you need your baby to be in a crib for your well-being as a mother and a person, then it's time to begin the transition.

The best way to make the transition is to involve Dad. Get your baby used to being put down to sleep by your husband. Wearing down, as discussed on page 52, is a technique that has worked well for us. When your baby is ready for bed (or you are ready for her to go to bed!), encourage your husband to wear her around the house in a baby sling until she falls asleep. Then ease her out of the sling into her crib once she is fully asleep. (Wait about twenty minutes after she falls asleep to be sure she is deeply asleep.) If you always nurse your little one to sleep, she is likely to want to be nursed back to sleep when she awakens. But if she gets used to Dad putting her to sleep, she's more likely to accept him putting her back to sleep when she awakens.

If your baby won't accept Dad's nighttime comforting, let her sleep in your bed for a couple of nights without you (you can sleep in another room). That way, she'll find Dad and not you when she wakes up. While this obviously won't be her preference, she'll gradually get used to being "father-nursed" back to sleep in whatever way your husband manages. Prepare him that this will take some creativity on his part (such as rocking and singing to her), since your baby is so used to going back to sleep at the breast.

Try these techniques for a couple of weeks, using your intuition and sensitivity as a guide. If they don't work, this probably means that your baby's desire to sleep with you comes from need (which can't be broken) rather than habit (which is easily broken). When this is the case, resume co-sleeping for a few weeks and then try this method again.

As a compromise, you might try a co-sleeper, as described on page 12.

☙

Getting Baby to Nap

Q *My ten-month-old refuses to take a morning nap and usually doesn't get more than a half-hour nap during the day. I've never just put him in his crib and let him cry, but I'm getting to that point! I know he must be exhausted, and I am, too. Help!*

A Both babies and parents need naps. Ten-month-old babies need at least a one-hour nap in the morning and a one- to two-hour snooze in the afternoon. Between one and two years, some babies drop the morning nap, but most still require one in the afternoon.

You can't force your baby to sleep, but you can create conditions that allow sleep to overtake him. Here are ways to encourage your reluctant napper to give it a rest:

- *Nap with him.* You probably look forward to your baby's naptime so you can "finally get something done." Resist this temptation. Naps are as important for you as they are for your infant.
- *Establish a routine.* To get him on a predictable nap schedule, set aside time in the morning and in the afternoon for napping. This will get your baby used to a consistent pattern.
- *Set the scene.* A few minutes before naptime, cuddle your baby in a dark, quiet room. Play soft music and

nestle together in a rocking chair, or lie down on a bed. This will set him up to expect sleep to follow. Once he's in a deep sleep (look for the limp-limb sign), either join him in a nap or ease him into his crib and slip away.

Baby Wants Only Midnight Meals

Q *Our eight-month-old isn't interested in breast-feeding during the day but wants to nurse all night. I'm too tired to do this!*

A Babies in their second six months of life often prefer to take their meals at night because they're too busy perfecting new and exciting motor skills during the day. By eight months most babies are sitting up, crawling, and grabbing. Exploration and play occupy much more of their time than ever before, and mealtimes are often forgotten until the family winds down for the night. In addition, it's common for babies of this age to practice their motor skills in the middle of the night. Once baby's up and about, she is apt to request a meal before falling back to sleep.

The best way to avoid nocturnal snacking is to get more milk into your baby during the daylight hours. Try nursing your baby every three hours during the day, even if you're not currently feeding her on a schedule. Or you can try nap nursing: Choose a couple of times during the day when you typically feel sleepy, say, 11:00 A.M. and 3:00 P.M. Lie down with your baby in a dark, quiet room. Getting your baby away from distractions may reawaken her nursing impulse just as the quiet nights do.

A couple of weeks of these scheduled daytime feedings should be enough to teach your baby that daytime is for both eating and playing—and that nighttime is for sleeping.

✑

Sleep-Sharing with a Wiggly Baby

Q *We share a bed with our ten-month-old. She has just started crawling and climbing, and I'm concerned she'll fall out of bed. I'm having her take naps on the floor now.*

A Every parent and child needs to work out a sleeping arrangement that allows everyone in the family to get a good night's sleep. However, a sleep setup that seems ideal for everyone may need to change as your baby reaches a new stage of development. Your baby has found some exciting new motor skills and wants to practice them at night, which is common in babies this age. Still, as normal as they are, these late-night antics are a nuisance for tired parents and can rob your baby of much-needed sleep.

You might consider trying what we call the "sidecar arrangement," a sleep strategy that has worked well in our family. This involves purchasing a particular type of crib known as a co-sleeper (see page 12), which attaches safely and snugly to the side of your bed. This gives both you and your baby your own space while keeping her well within nursing and nurturing distance. In addition, it will force her to crawl over and wake you before she can get to the edge of the bed, where she could fall. As an added benefit, once your baby gets used to having her own sleep space in the co-sleeper, she will have less trouble moving into a traditional two-railed crib or toddler bed down the road.

⌘

Foods That Keep Children Awake

Q *Are there any foods that keep babies up at night?*

A It's no surprise that foods containing caffeine top the list of "sleepless" menus for adults and children alike. Caffeine stimulates the production of adrenal hormones, which induce higher heart and breathing rates and increased urinary output and stomach acid production. Basically caffeine's effect on the body is the direct opposite of sleep. The degree to which caffeine interferes with sleep varies with the individual; some adults and children are more sensitive to caffeine than others.

Coffee, colas, and tea are typically high in caffeine, as are many cold and headache medicines (contrary to popular belief, chocolate contains little caffeine). Of course, it's unlikely that you're feeding any of these to your baby, but you should know that caffeine can pass through the milk of a breastfeeding mother and thus disrupt a baby's sleep. Caffeine enters breast milk in such small quantities, however, that typically a nursing mom would have to drink six cups of coffee to have a noticeable effect on her baby. Still, the amount that causes problems does vary from person to person, and every breastfeeding mother needs to be aware of how much caffeine she can consume without affecting her baby.

Solid Foods and Sound Sleep

Q *Do certain foods help babies sleep better at night? I've heard that solids can make babies sleepy.*

A Parents desperate to get their babies to sleep longer will try anything, including giving them solids before bedtime. We call this the "filler-food fallacy."

In research studies, four-month-olds who were slipped some solids at bedtime did not sleep any better at night than four-month-olds who weren't. Yet many mothers in my practice insist that their babies sleep more soundly when they feed them a bit of rice cereal or mashed bananas before bedtime. So if you have a frequent night waker over the age of five months (children younger than that shouldn't be eating solids), feeding him solids at bedtime is worth a try.

The best sleepytime snack for baby is breast milk, which contains a natural sleep-inducing protein. And baby isn't the only one being lulled to sleep here. The act of nursing induces the production of the relaxation hormone prolactin in Mom, making breastfeeding the absolute best bedtime activity for both mother and child.

෨

When Nighttime Feedings
Take Over

Q *My daughter, who will be one year old next week, has never slept through the night without waking for a feeding. She's never taken a bottle, so I've had to breast-feed her every time she awakens, usually while lying with her on a mattress on the floor in her room. How do I break this habit? I've tried not giving her the breast when she awakens, but after listening to her cry for fifteen minutes, I feel like crying myself and always give in. What should I do?*

A Because you are a sensitive, caring mother, you are unable to fall into the often-given "let your baby cry it out" advice. You are responding as any nurturing mother would—comforting your baby back to sleep.

Don't feel that your baby is manipulating you or that you are "giving in." You are responding from your heart, according to your maternal instinct. It's easy for others to tell you to let your baby cry it out because they are not your child's mother, and they are not there at 3:00 A.M.

The goal of nighttime parenting is to develop a sleeping arrangement that gets both you and your baby the best night's sleep possible and gives your daughter a sense of security. If your baby can easily drift back to sleep after night nursing and you do not feel sleep deprived the next day, this is the best arrangement.

If, however, you are weary the next day, you need to make a change. Try having her sleep next to you, either in your bed or in a co-sleeper (see page 12). Then you will be more likely to drift back to sleep after feeding her. To encourage her to resettle without nursing, get your baby used to being put down to sleep by Dad (see page 74). Once she is used to Dad, she's more likely to accept him helping her back to sleep in the night when she awakens.

Baby Won't Sleep Alone

Q *My one-year-old can't go to sleep alone, and he wakes up at least two or three times during the night. He shares a bed with my husband and me, and we'd like to continue this arrangement. I have a bedtime routine (changing him into his pj's and reading stories), which I usually begin when he shows signs of being tired. The problem is, he can't fall asleep unless I'm lying next to him and he often awakens when I try to get up. Now his night-time problems have extended into the daytime, and he won't nap unless my childcare provider lies down with him. I'd like to teach him ways to soothe himself to sleep. What should I do?*

A It's always helpful to know why your child acts the way he does—and the best way to do that is to imagine yourself in his shoes. At night your son is in physical contact with his favorite people in the whole world. He's used to sleeping first-class and he's not excited about the change.

Still, there comes a time for nighttime independence. To foster a healthy sleep attitude in your child, you want him to feel that sleep is a pleasant and fearless state—which is why you don't want to succumb to the often-given advice "put your baby in a room, put cotton in your ears, and let him cry it out." What you want to do is get your baby used to falling asleep under different conditions. Ask your caregiver to continue lying with him until he falls asleep and get Dad to do the same from time to time. Once he has become accustomed to various people putting him to sleep, teach him how to stay asleep without a person lying next to him. Use favorite attachment objects, like his favorite teddy bear or blanket. Try using a continuous-play tape recording of lullabies or even a medley of your own voice singing his favorite songs so that he learns to associate these sounds with sleep.

If he still needs a partner to get to sleep, try a co-sleeper (see page 12) setup. This should give you and your baby your own sleeping space yet keep him close enough to be able to sleep. Keep a consistent bedtime routine, including a bath, reading stories, and prolonged cuddle time. On days when you are away for many hours, expect your baby to prolong the nighttime ritual as he tries to reconnect with you to make up for the touch time he missed during the day.

✑

Sleep Needs at Different Ages

Q *My daughter is thirteen months old and sleeps from 10:00 P.M. until 8:00 A.M. She also has two forty-five-minute naps during the day. Is this enough sleep? How much sleep should a baby get at different ages?*

A Most thirteen-month-olds sleep around twelve hours a day, including naps. Your daughter is only a little bit short of the average. If she seems well rested, this may be enough sleep for her. If she seems tired or irritable or nods off to sleep frequently during the day, she needs more sleep. Below is a chart of average sleeping times for children of different ages.

Age	Hours per Day
birth to 3 months	14 to 18
3 to 6 months	14 to 16
6 months to 2 years	12 to 14
2 to 5 years	10 to 12

A 10:00 P.M. bedtime would once have been considered late for a thirteen-month-old. Modern lifestyles have pushed bedtimes later, especially among working couples, who might not get home until seven in the evening and prefer that their baby take a late-afternoon nap and be well rested for quality time in the evening. Some parents prefer the later bedtimes for baby so that they can get that extra hour of sleep in the morning. Other parents want an earlier bedtime so that they can get in some baby-free couple time in the evening.

Make your own family's rules. Find the bedtime that works for you and your baby. If 10:00 P.M. lights-out keeps your baby rested and suits your schedule, stay with it.

Discouraging Nighttime Nursing

Q *We didn't intend to be a "family bed" family, but we found that sharing sleep worked best for everyone. Although I'd like to continue sleep-sharing, I would prefer that my one-year-old son didn't wake up to nurse at night. He refuses to lie next to me and let me soothe him back to sleep by rubbing his back. Instead, he pounces on me and tries to nurse. Is my child old enough to understand that my breasts sleep when I sleep?*

A You have learned a valuable lesson in parenting: You have to keep working to find a style of parenting (daytime and nighttime) that works for everyone. By being open to various sleeping arrangements, you found one that allows you all to sleep better.

Look at your present dilemma from your baby's viewpoint: He sleeps next to his favorite comfort food, only inches away from his eager mouth. Babies don't realize that mothers need sleep; they merely want what is in their own best interest—which is to night-nurse.

It is normal for a one-year-old to wake once or twice a night to nurse. This is fine as long as you're not waking up in the morning exhausted. But if you start resenting going to bed because it's more like work than rest, you need to make a change.

Here are ways to convince your little nocturnal gourmand that nighttime is for sleeping rather than nursing:

- *Fill him up with more nursings during the day.* Many toddlers get so busy during the day that they forget to nurse. Then they try to make up for those missed nursings at night.
- *Wake him up for an extended nursing before you go to sleep.*
- *Get him used to going to bed by methods other than nursing.* Try wearing him in a baby sling around the house until he is fully asleep, and then ease him into your bed. If Dad takes over this part of the bedtime routine, your baby will learn to associate him with falling asleep. Then when your baby wakes up at night, he's more likely to accept Dad putting him back to sleep.
- *Increase the physical distance between the two of you at night.* Try the co-sleeper (see page 12). Sometimes this will dampen a baby's desire to night-nurse. If your baby persists in wanting to night-nurse, move to another room

and let baby sleep next to Dad for a few nights. This will teach your child that he can get through the night without nursing. (Back off after a week's try if this causes too much crying. Night-nursing may still be a need for your baby, and unlike a habit, a need is not easily broken.)

By eighteen months, your baby will be old enough to handle some nighttime frustration. If he is still waking more than you can handle, play dead when he awakens, and let Dad do the honors for a few nights (he can offer a drink of water and walk baby back to sleep). Your baby will still cry, but that's okay. He's not being left to cry alone, and he'll learn to limit his night nursing.

None of these steps will work, however, if your baby's excessive waking is due to a physical problem (such as teething, a developmental spurt, illness, GER, and food or environmental sensitivities). Once you address this problem, you can look forward to better sleep for yourself and your baby.

Finally, remember that it's okay for baby to nurse once or twice at night quite a while longer. Night nursing won't last forever. The time spent in your arms, at your breast, and in your bed is a relatively short period in the total life of your child. Still, the memories of love and availability will last a lifetime.

☙

Getting Baby to Sleep at Day Care

Q My fifteen-month-old daughter will be entering day care part-time, and I'm concerned about naptime. At home she either nurses herself to sleep or I take her for a drive. How can I teach her another way to go to sleep?

A The first thing to do is talk to your childcare provider about how she can create an environment for your daughter that mimics her home environment as closely as possible. It will also be less confusing for your baby if the childcare provider can use a parenting style that is similar to yours. Even if she can't nurse your infant to sleep, your baby can still be lulled to sleep in her arms, provided your baby is her only charge. Nursing is about comforting, not just breastfeeding, especially at this age. Anyone can nurse a baby to sleep in this sense. Explain to your baby-sitter that your infant is used to being nursed to sleep and that you would like her to go to sleep in her arms, accompanied by rocking or singing or with someone lying next to her if possible.

A nap-inducing trick we've used successfully with our children is one we call "wearing down." Show the child-care provider how to wear your baby in a carrier—prefer-ably a sling-type carrier—as naptime nears. Babies love to fall asleep in a sling. Once your baby is in a deep sleep, her childcare provider can ease her out of the sling and into the crib.

"Nursing" a baby to sleep is one of the best methods you can use at naptime. It creates a healthy sleep attitude by providing a safe and loving environment in which to fall asleep and will help your baby to grow up knowing that sleep is a pleasant and fearless state.

⊘

Diaper Changes at Night

Q *When my baby awakens at night, could it be because she wants a diaper change? Is it always necessary to change her diaper at this time?*

A Some babies are bothered by wet diapers at night, but most are not. If your baby sleeps through wet diapers, there is no need to awaken her for a change, unless she is prone to diaper rash. If you are using cloth diapers, double-diapering your baby may lessen the sensation of wetness. Nighttime bowel movements do require a change.

If your baby is bothered by wet diapers, here's how to get yourself and your baby a longer stretch of uninterrupted sleep. Change your baby's diaper right before or right after her bedtime feeding. If you nurse her down to sleep and she usually has a bowel movement right after you feed her (as many breastfeeding babies do), you'll need to change her immediately after the feeding. If her regular stool pattern is not to have a bowel movement after a feeding, change her before the last feeding. If baby is sleeping in your bed, keep an extra supply of diapers and baby wipes within easy reaching distance. A night-light or room light on a low dimmer makes it easier to identify baby's diapering needs. A flannel-backed rubber pad under baby will protect your mattress from nighttime accidents.

Here are some common reasons that babies wake up at night:

- *Hunger.* Expect your infant to wake up for one or two night feedings during the first six months.
- *Teething pain.* A wet sheet under baby's head, a telltale drool rash on the cheeks and chin, tender and swollen gums, and waking in pain are often indications that teething is the cause of night waking, especially between five and seven months.
- *Stuffy nose.* Tiny babies need clear nasal passages to breathe. Newborns are especially restless if their nose is congested. Environmental irritants, such as dust from blankets or fuzzy toys, mother's perfume or hair spray, animal dander, and cigarette smoke, are common irritants that lead to stuffy noses and consequent night waking.
- *Irritating sleepwear.* You may have to experiment with cotton versus polyester sleepers to see which type is most comfortable for your baby.

- *Developmental changes.* Expect bouts of night waking
  when baby is going through a major developmental
  change, such as sitting up, crawling, or walking. Sometimes the beginning sitter will try to sit up at night and
  will wake himself up when he topples over.

Usually by the end of the first year, as babies begin to
enjoy more deep sleep, they are able to sleep through many
of these potential disturbances, and the whole family
begins to enjoy a longer stretch of uninterrupted sleep.

Nighttime Parenting
Twins

Q *What advice can you give parents of twins who are
both nonsleepers?*

A Many parents in our pediatrics practice who are
blessed with multiples describe the first year with their
babies as a "blur." Much of this feeling is due to twice as
much night waking. Try these sleep-inducing tricks:

- Instead of putting your twins in separate bassinets in the
  early months, place them side by side or face-to-face in

the same bassinet. After all, they have been womb mates for nine months. If they don't settle well sleeping side by side, put them in separate bassinets. You could also try a bedside co-sleeper for each baby (see page 12).

- Double-team for nighttime parenting. In nighttime-parenting one baby, nighttime fathering is an option. With multiples, it's a must. As one tired father of twins in our practice boasted: "Our babies have two mothers. She's the milk mother and I'm the hairy mother." What he meant was that in caring for twins, the mother-father roles are not so clear-cut. Except for breastfeeding, all the high-maintenance tasks of infant care can be shared by the father. Even though fathers can't breastfeed, they can still "nurse," in the sense of comfort.

- Get help so you can rest. For parents of twins, household help is not a luxury, it's a necessity. If your friends ask what they can do for you, ask them to bring a meal or do a bit of housekeeping. With twins, you're going to need to be doubly organized. Do what you have to do and delegate the rest.

- Try a technique we call "carrying double." Carried babies cry less. Get two sling-type carriers (one for Mom and one for Dad) and frequently wear your babies out for a walk. Motion settles babies, and oftentimes the more settled babies are during the day, the longer stretches they sleep at night.

- Try to get the twins on a predictable nap schedule. Choose the two times during the day when you are the most tired and nap with them.

- Continue to let Dad help put the twins to bed. This capitalizes on the principle of sleep associations—the way a baby goes to sleep is the way he expects to be put back to sleep. If your infants always associate going to sleep with breastfeeding, they will always want to be breastfed back to sleep. "Father nursing" is the key to nighttime-parenting twins.

- Tank them up with more feedings during the day, so that they learn that daytime is for eating and playing and nighttime is for sleeping. As your twins get older, they'll often get so busy playing with each other during the day that they'll forget to eat and will want to make up for these missed feedings at night.

- Try continuous-play tape recordings of favorite lullabies at bedtime. When they awaken and hear the familiar tunes, they may resettle by themselves.

Be prepared to juggle various sleeping arrangements to get all family members the best night's sleep.

✑

Matching Sibling Naps

Q *I have a toddler and a newborn who nap at different times. Is there any way I can get them on the same nap schedule?*

A We tell parents that they should nap when their babies nap. This becomes virtually impossible, however, when an infant and a toddler compete for your attention. Most often, your older child will demand your undivided attention when your baby is napping, because this is when you have your hands free—and most toddlers notice this.

Consequently, it's easier to schedule some of your newborn's naptimes to coincide with your toddler's rather than vice versa. Whenever your toddler takes his nap, lie down with your baby and start to transition her to sleep (see page 51). Hopefully, your toddler already has a regular nap schedule that the baby can adjust to. This adjustment may take a week or two, but if you do this consistently, you should be able to get them to match up on at least one nap per day. Once you achieve that, savor the sleep time! You need that rest more than the house needs cleaning. Pick out once or twice each day when you are the most tired (say, 11:00 A.M. and 3:00 P.M.) and nap with your children, one on each side of you. Even if your toddler doesn't nap, he will learn that this is quiet time.

If you have an infant who is a frequent night waker, a single nap during the day isn't adequate for her. If this is the case, you need to seek help. Parents must learn to ration their time and attention according to their children's needs and their available energy. Whenever possible, Mom and Dad should work in shifts, with Dad taking care of the toddler while Mom and baby nap. When it's not possible, maybe you can draft a trusted relative or neighbor to come by and watch your older child once a day. If your toddler is more than two years old, enroll him in a playgroup for a few afternoons each week.

⌘

The Overcrowded Family Bed

Q *Our six-year-old and our two-year-old have both made our bed their regular sleeping spot. And while we enjoy the many benefits of the family bed, we'd like to get the kids to sleep in their own room. What's the best way to accomplish this?*

A Bed sharing, or nighttime parenting, is especially valuable for parents who have little time with their children during the day. It allows them to reconnect at night, compensating for touch time missed during the day. It's important, however, to find a sleeping arrangement that works for the whole family. We've found that bed sharing works best if there is only one child involved. Otherwise, the kids tend to take over and the adults feel squeezed. One way to deal with overcrowding in the family bed is to put a futon or mattress on the floor in your room. Encourage your six-year-old to sleep in this "special bed," allowing him the security of feeling close to you at night but getting him used to separate sleeping. Later, move your two-year-old into the special bed next to his brother. When they are both comfortable with the arrangement, move the special bed into their own room. Since they're already sleeping in the same bed, it should be easy to ease them into a shared sleeping arrangement in another room.

☞

Is Three a Crowd?

Q *Will the family bed ruin our sex life and leave us with no privacy?*

A Contrary to contemporary Western social beliefs, sex and babies can mix. Very young babies are not too aware of their surroundings and don't understand what is going on. For those reasons, lovemaking in the family bed is seldom a problem when your infant is only a few months old.

Please note, however, that because of the sacrifices that will be made in the privacy department, the choice to bring baby into bed needs to be made by both Mom and Dad. If Dad feels he's competing with his baby for Mom's night-time attentions, he may start to resent the newcomer. Talk it out before you try the family bed, and check in with each other from time to time to see if it's still working for both of you.

Of course, as baby gets older, parents find themselves sexually inhibited in the presence of their sleeping child. When this happens try these tactics to keep your bed family territory and your love life active:

• Let baby sleep in her own crib (or bed) at first and then bring her into your bed when she awakens later in the night.

- Explore the idea that the master bedroom is not the only place in the house suited for lovemaking. If baby is sleeping in your bed when the mood hits, either move baby or move yourselves. A candlelit walk-in closet and other areas of the home are potential "love chambers."
- Use the "go watch cartoons" approach for the toddler or older child. Or ask the older child to leave your bedroom by simply saying, "Mommy and Daddy need to be alone right now."
- Find time for intimacy during the day. You may find that morning or daytime sex is easier and more enjoyable. Besides, during the early months, most mothers are too tired at night to do anything but sleep. As one mother put it, "I need my sleep more than he needs sex."

New parents often wonder, "When will our lives get back to normal?" We've got news for you: Once you have a baby, this *is* your normal life! Learning to juggle nighttime parenting and lovemaking is just one challenge of being a parent and a spouse.

🙢

How to Get Your Toddler to Go to Bed—and Stay There

Q *My twenty-two-month-old, who sleeps in a toddler bed, has taken to running out of his room and into our bedroom at all hours of the night. Short of locking him in his room, which I do not want to do, how can I get him to stay put and go to sleep?*

A It's normal for toddlers to periodically run out of their room and into their parents' bedroom at night. This is a normal developmental stage, though, admittedly, these night visits can be exhausting.

To give your child extra nighttime security without disrupting your sleep, put a futon, mattress, or sleeping bag at the foot of your bed and then establish this rule: "You can come into Mommy and Daddy's room at night if you like and sleep in your special bed, but you must tiptoe as quietly as a mouse and not wake up Mommy and Daddy. Mommy and Daddy need our sleep, or we will be cranky the next day."

To entice your child to stay in his own room and bed, try the following:

- Leave a glass of water at his bedside in case he wakes up thirsty.

- Put on a continuous-play tape recording of you singing a medley of lullabies or favorite songs.
- Install a dim night-light in his room.
- Make his bed so attractive that he wants to stay in it by letting him pick out a special comforter, sheets, or sleeping bag, and allowing him to bring his favorite toys under the covers with him.

⳽

Banning the Nighttime Binky

Q *My two-year-old still uses a pacifier to sleep. I think it's time to wean him. Do you agree? If so, what's the easiest and least traumatic way to do this?*

A In the early months, the sucking action is an activity that babies associate with comfort and sleep. Later in life, many hard-charging toddlers will resort to sucking to unwind after a long day of exploring and growing. As a result, many pacifier babies grow into toddlers with a rubber-nipple nighttime routine.

Still, there comes a time when you must "pull the plug." The trouble with using a pacifier as a sleep aid is that overuse can result in overbite, when a child's upper teeth protrude far in front of his lower teeth.

To see if it's time for a binky ban, check for overbite by rubbing your finger along your son's teeth as he sleeps. If you detect the beginning of an overbite, it's time to wean him off this bedtime habit.

The best methods for all types of weaning are gradual and involve substitutes. At first, continue letting him drift off to sleep with his pacifier. Once he's deep in dreamland, ease the pacifier out of his mouth. If he has a strong sleep-pacifier association, he may need a comfort object to help him back to sleep when he wakes in the middle of the night. You can introduce some alternative non-oral pacifiers, like a cuddly teddy bear or favorite blanket. In time, the substituted item should replace the pacifier as your child's bedtime companion of choice.

Pacifiers are useful tools for comforting baby, but they should be used in addition to parental nurturing, not as a substitute. You should be your baby's primary comfort tool. Nonetheless, if your baby insists on sleeping with a pacifier, please observe these two safety rules:

- Avoid making your own pacifier out of a cotton-stuffed bottle nipple. Baby may suck the cotton through the hole.
- Resist the temptation to sweeten the offering by dipping the pacifier in honey or syrup, as this could contribute to tooth decay.

❧

Tips for Tired Moms

Q *When my three-month-old wakes up at night, I relish our "mommy-son" time. But the next day I'm a living zombie. Any tips for me to feel more rested?*

A Many mothers report mixed feelings about those frequent night nursings. On the one hand, it's a special uninterrupted time of mother-baby togetherness that will pass all too soon. It's a time when you can totally enjoy this special closeness with your infant unencumbered by the distractions of the day. On the other hand, all this nighttime giving can wear thin after a while, especially if you are feeling sleep-deprived during the day. You will find that, like all parenting styles, nighttime parenting requires a balance between what is good for baby and what is good for mommy. If trying to be the perfect nighttime parent means being a grouchy mommy during the day, that is not good for either of you. Here's how to get close to your baby and get your rest, too.

First, develop a sleeping arrangement that allows you to comfort and nurse your baby at night without fully awakening. This is why many mothers choose to co-sleep with their babies. When baby is nestled right next to Mom, the pair develops what is called nighttime harmony. They get their sleep cycles in sync with one another, so they both wake up during the stage of light sleep and both sleep during the stage of deep sleep. It's not so much frequent night waking that wears moms out as it is being awakened from a state of deep sleep. Within a few weeks or months, you should be able to develop this nighttime harmony. If having baby sleep close to you causes you and/or your baby to wake up more frequently, try a bedside co-sleeper (see page 12). Each mother-infant pair seems to have a critical sleeping distance where they get the most sleep. Try to arrive at the sleeping arrangement that gets you and your infant the best night's sleep.

Have a realistic appraisal of how much night nursing you can do and still feel semi-rested the next day. Then honor your mate with his share of nighttime fathering, so that baby gets used to being put down to sleep and put back to sleep by another set of sensitive arms.

Nap with your baby a couple of times during the day to make up for the missed sleep during the night. Also, babies who get used to a consistent naptime routine tend to sleep longer at night. Try music to sleep by or tape recordings of waterfalls or ocean sounds, or play a medley of lullabies on a continuous-play tape recorder.

Since you enjoy this special time at night, treasure it while it lasts, but try to use the methods above to get yourself a few extra hours of quality sleep. By four months of age, most babies start having more mature sleep cycles and sleep for longer stretches.

⅏

Snoring and Sleep Apnea

Q *My two-year-old son was on an apnea monitor until he was twelve months old. Now he snores almost every time he falls asleep. Should I be concerned?*

A It is unlikely that your son's snoring is related to the use of an apnea monitor during the first year. Apnea—that is, stop-breathing or slow-breathing episodes—can have many causes. Central apnea, which occurs during the first twelve months, is usually due to immaturity in the breathing center of the brain; this often self-corrects with time and maturity. At age two obstructive apnea may appear; cause by a partial obstruction in the airways. This is due to structural abnormalities in the nasal passages or in the back of the throat. A child's snoring is usually a sign of some obstruction that needs to be removed.

Watch your child sleep. If he experiences stretches of ten to fifteen seconds when he doesn't breathe followed by an intense catch-up breath, report this to your doctor. Sleep apnea and snoring at night may be due to enlarged tonsils. During the day, the tonsils do not compromise the airway, but at night the airway relaxes and narrows, and more effort is required to force the air through. This is what produces the snoring noise.

Have your child's nasal passages and throat examined by your pediatrician. If your doctor is unable to detect a structural problem, be sure your child's sleeping environment is free of allergens—including dust collectors or animal dander—which can cause nighttime stuffiness and result in noisy breathing. Besides removing potential allergens, a HEPA bedroom air purifier can help eliminate dust. HEPA filters are efficient in filtering out almost 100 percent of airborne allergens and danders. Encouraging different sleep positions for your child may also be helpful. Sleeping on his side or stomach may relieve your child's snoring.

If the snoring persist's after a medical exam and after making changes in your child's sleeping enviromnent, don't worry. Most likely your son's heavy nighttime breathing will self-correct with time.

⌘

Removing a Child's Adenoids

Q *Our two-year-old son has extremely large adenoid glands. Our pediatrician told us not to worry, but the adenoids bother my child's breathing, especially at night. He snores constantly and is very tired the next day. Should I be concerned?*

A It sounds like your son's adenoids should be removed. Large adenoids obstruct a child's breathing more during sleep than in waking hours. Sleep relaxes the airway so that it becomes more narrow, making the obstruction worse. Sleep apnea, which your child most likely has, is one absolute criterion for removing obstructive tonsils and/or adenoids.

Sleep apnea interferes with a child's overall growth and well-being. Children alternate between light and deep sleep, and when their airway becomes obstructed, they often awaken with a startle from lack of air. This causes an adrenaline rush and revs up the child's nervous system at night, interfering with sleep.

Incidentally, the nighttime adrenaline rush also causes the bladder to empty. So as an added perk, you will probably notice more nighttime dryness once your child's adenoids come out.

Let your pediatrician know that you are worried about your child's adenoids and sleep apnea, and ask for a referral to an ear, nose, and throat (ENT) specialist.

ᔕ

Coping with an Early Riser

Q *You'd think Christmas morning came every day at our house. Our toddler is up at 5:00 A.M. without fail. How can we get him to sleep longer so that we can catch some more shut-eye?*

A Purists would say children should be allowed to wake at dawn or whenever their internal clocks dictate. Still, that's easy to say when you're not the one living with a walking, talking alarm clock. For already overtaxed and overtired parents, that early wake-up call can be just too much.

Babies and young children often don't have a mature sense of time. Often, the slightest bit of light coming in through the window as dawn breaks is enough to wake a child, especially if it coincides with a fragile point in the child's sleep cycle.

Here are some ways to keep your child snoozing longer:

- Set rules for older siblings to keep their sound levels low in the morning.
- Hang room-darkening opaque curtains in your child's room to prolong the dark of night.
- Give your son an alarm clock "just like Mommy and Daddy's." Tell him that he can get out of bed when the alarm goes off, the same way Mommy and Daddy do.
- Leave a box of quiet toys by your son's bed, so he has something to occupy him if he awakens before you do.
- Leave a nutritious snack on a bedside table to keep the hungry riser satisfied until breakfast.

⌔

Getting a Preschooler to Sleep in Her Own Bed

Q   *Our two-year-old wakes up in the middle of the night and either demands to sleep in our bed or insists that my wife go sleep with her in her room. How can we break this habit?*

A First decide whether your child's desire to sleep with you is a habit or need (a parent can tell the difference). Nighttime can be scary for youngsters, so if you are in doubt, consider it a need. Contact at night gives you and your child a chance to reconnect. The desire for nighttime contact may be particularly strong if your child had little contact with you during the day. The key is to find a compromise that meets both your need for privacy and sleep and your child's need for attachment and security.

Lie down with your child in her room and parent her to sleep with a story, a back rub, and some cuddle time. Also set nighttime rules, as your two-year-old needs to understand the importance of not disturbing your sleep. Put a futon or mattress at the foot of your bed. Explain that if she wakes up, she can come and sleep in her "special bed." If she needs comfort during the night, tell her to tiptoe in quietly and slip into her special bed without waking Mommy or Daddy. Eventually your daughter will spend more time in her own bed, resorting to the special bed only during times of stress—a change in schools or friends, a move, or any of life's little upsets that can disturb a child's sleep.

Above all, don't feel you are spoiling your child or that she is psychologically disturbed because she can't sleep on her own. Many emotionally healthy children simply enjoy the nighttime security of sleeping close to their parents. When it comes down to it, the time your youngster spends in your room (or in your bed) is relatively short. Still, it encourages a positive lifelong attitude about bedtime, conveying that sleep is a pleasant rather than fearful state to enter.

❧

Night Terrors

Q *Our daughter (age two and a half) wakes up screaming almost every night. She sleeps in our bed and tosses and turns a lot, but we are unable to comfort her. When she was eleven months old, she was diagnosed with an autoimmune neutropenic disorder and underwent bone marrow testing. Could this hospital experience be the cause of her terrors?*

A Night terrors can be frightening for parents to witness. A child with typical nigh terrors awakens from a state of deep sleep. She may sit up in bed, let out a piercing scream, and even appear pale and terrified. She may stare with eyes wide open at an imaginary object, cry incoherently, breathe heavily, perspire, and (as you have found) be completely unreceptive to attempts to console her. The episodes can last five to ten minutes, and then the child usually falls back into a deep, calm sleep.

A child who has a nightmare, on the other hand, fully awakens, remembers the scary dream, and has difficulty reentering sleep without nighttime parenting. But children with night terrors don't remember this bizarre nighttime activity because they aren't fully awake during the episodes. As a result, children with night terrors are unlikely to develop a fearful attitude about sleep or to seem sleep-deprived the next day.

It is quite possible that your daughter's hospital experience triggered her terrors. A bone marrow test is a traumatic event for anyone. Your child was at an impressionable age when the procedure occurred, and she may be subconsciously replaying the memory in her sleep. Still, there are many theories about what causes night terrors.

Remember that a child's developing mind is like an expanding file cabinet. Right now, your daughter's hospital experience is taking up a large file in her memory. The best you can do is to plant pleasant experiences in her mind that will gradually overshadow the unpleasant ones.

It sounds like you are giving your child the best therapy there is: your love and availability. Initiate some quiet bedtime rituals—a pleasant game, a relaxing story, a back rub, and soothing music. Children often replay before-bed rituals in their sleep, so pleasant and relaxing bedtime routines are less likely to trigger nightmares or night terrors.

Changing Bedtime Routines

Q *I have a hard time getting my two-year-old daughter to sleep. We finally established a good routine where I stay with her for fifteen to twenty minutes until she falls asleep (it used to take an hour or more). But lately we've started a new round of nightly battles to get her to go to bed. Over the last three month there have been changes in our lives: We moved across country away from my parents and her navy dad started sailing again after being home for the first two years of her life. What can I do?*

A When drastic changes occur in a family's routine, it's normal to expect sleep problems to occur. The combination of moving across country away from her grandparents and separation from Dad is bound to keep any two-year-old awake at night. This is not the time to be tough. Your daughter needs the nighttime security of the one attachment person who remains constant in her life—her mother. Many military moms find it works best to have a preschool child sleep in their room or even in their bed while Dad is away.

Lie down together on your bed until your child falls asleep, and then get up to resume your evening activities. When you retire for the night, you can leave her in your bed, move her to a mattress at the foot of your bed, or transfer her to her own room. Ignore the "sleep trainers" who advise you to let her cry it out. Your child has reason for nighttime insecurities right now, and if you respect them, you'll both probably sleep a lot better while Dad is away.

♋

The Bedtime of
a Thousand Excuses

Q *My two-year-old has an eight o'clock bedtime, but he has a hundred excuses to stay up, from a drink of water to one last pee to bogeymen in his closet. He's often awake until 9:00 or 10:00 P.M. Where should I draw the line?*

A Decades ago, when most Americans lived in rural settings, the family got up early, worked together for most of the day, and went to bed at the same time, usually in the early evening. Today's parents, especially if both work outside the home, don't have as much time to spend with their children during the day. As a result, many children balk at bedtime and demand more of their parents' attention at night. Children are even more likely to rebel against their bedtimes following upsetting changes in their routines, such as the arrival of a new baby or a change in childcare providers. These are times when they need more nurturing parent time. Keep this in mind, especially when you are negotiating with your toddler night owl. Rather than being obstinate and stubborn, your child is actually angling for more time with you. Take it as the compliment that it is.

Sleep is a state that has to come naturally. Parents must create an environment that will encourage the child to go to bed on readily. The most effective way to do that is to develop a consistent bedtime ritual.

If you can get your child to associate certain activities with bedtime, he may actually insist on turning in at that time, since preschoolers cherish their routines. It helps if your bedtime ritual includes some sleepy, comfortable activities, such as a warm bath, a back rub, a soothing story, or a gradual dimming of the lights. We recommend that parents share the tucking-in routine at bedtime so that child is used to this nightly ritual with both parents.

Try these strategies for getting your child to go to bed more willingly:

- Play the back-rub game. "Plant a garden" on your child's back, using different touches to indicate different fruits and vegetables. Gradually lighten your stroke as you smooth out the garden "soil."
- Lie in bed with your child as you read him his bedtime story. Stay there with him until he's sound asleep.
- Play a continuously looped recording of one of your child's favorite stories. Or make a tape of yourself reading a bedtime story to be used when you're unable to be there in person.
- Choose bedtime stories that you would not mind reading over and over. Books that emphasize repetitive or rhyming sounds are comforting and work best.
- Schedule an hour or two of outdoor exercise during the day. Some children have trouble going to sleep because they are not tired. Exercise may use up enough energy so that the child naturally relaxes as bedtime approaches.
- Start the bedtime ritual earlier (say, around 7:00 P.M.)

and avoid any rambunctious play after this time. A later bedtime might be more realistic for your family, but in general, consistent, earlier bedtimes are usually better for kids.

☙

Staying Up Late

Q *My two-year-old refuses to go to sleep until we do—usually around 11:00 P.M. or midnight—and we have the worst time waking her up in the morning. How can we get her to bed earlier without a fight?*

A Bedtime procrastination ranks high among parents' complaints. The many excuses preschool children come up with to delay bedtime are really an expression of their desire to spend more time with Mom and Dad rather than an unwillingness to go to sleep. We've noticed that the busier and more preoccupied we are during the day, the more our children lobby for quality time at night.

To get your child to sleep earlier and have more "couple time" in the evening, be sure your daughter is tired. Wear her out with exercise late in the afternoon. Establish a set bedtime say, 8:00 P.M. and begin your winding-down ritual an hour beforehand. Using the same routine every night will condition your youngster that sleep is expected to follow.

Start with a quiet game, followed by a soothing bath

and a calming story. Choose a story based on your own childhood or use the child's favorite movie characters: Pocahontas and John Smith went fishing and they caught one fish, two fish, three fish . . ." Sometimes it may take thirty fish to get your child to sleep. (Counting stories worked well for us, and fish stories have been Sears family favorites for years!)

Your goal is to make your bedtime ritual so loving and cuddly that your child prefers it to the activities she would do if she stayed awake. Sometimes a child is reluctant to go to sleep in her own bedroom because it signals the end of the day. If this is the case, parent her to sleep in your bed, then move her into her own room when you retire.

Here are some more time-tested ways to help children go to sleep and stay asleep:

- *Construct a peaceful day.* Children, like adults, may experience sleepless nights from daytime worry. Take an inventory of stressful situations that may occur in your child's life at school, day care, or at home and work to eliminate them. If you suspect your child is worried about something that happened during the day, talk it out in a reassuring way before bedtime.
- *Eliminate caffeine-containing foods.* Colas, tea, and even some medications may contain caffeine that can keep children awake.
- *Turn off scary television.* Witnessing violence—even on a seemingly harmless program, such as the evening news—can be especially upsetting to children. Even cartoons can cause nightmares. Children often replay and are awakened by disturbing scenes in their dreams.
- *Wind down before bed.* An hour or two before bedtime begin to wind your child down. This is not the time for

wrestling matches or games that excite the mind and rev up the body.

- *Strive for a consistent bedtime.* Consistency may be impractical for many families, but try to maintain a reasonably consistent, predictable bedtime for your child.
- *Establish a bedtime routine.* Children develop patterns of association when they participate in regular events, and a calming bedtime ritual can help set the stage for a peaceful night's sleep. The routine you create with your child may include a warm bath, teeth brushing, reading a story, and singing a song.
- *Expect procrastination.* Kids quickly learn that bedtime is the one time of day when they have their parents' undivided attention, so they try to prolong this time together as much as possible. Rather than regarding bedtime as a task, consider it an opportunity to reconnect with your child.
- *Parent your child to bed.* Many children love to have Mom or Dad lie down next to them and sing or snuggle them to sleep. In fact, we've found this to be one of the best five-minute investments to increase the chances of getting a full night's sleep.

Resources for Childcare Products and Information

Parenting and Pediatric Information

www.parenting.com. An informative Web site on parenting issues. Dr. Bill and Martha Sears answer parenting questions and host frequent chats and workshops.

www.AskDrSears.com. A comprehensive Web site on health-care information for infants and children.

Baby Carriers

A soft baby carrier is one of the most useful parenting products you and your baby will enjoy. Consult the following resources for information on sling-type carriers and step-by-step instructions on using a sling.

The Original BabySling 800-421-0526 or
www.originalbabysling.com or www.nojo.com

Crown Crafts Infant Products
310-763-8100 or www.crowncraftsinfantproducts.com

www.AskDrSears.com   Visit our store.

Bedside Co-Sleepers

A bedside co-sleeper lets baby and parents sleep close to one another yet still have their own space. This criblike bed safely attaches to the parents' bed.

Arm's Reach Co-Sleeper 800-954-9353 or 818-879-9353 or www.armsreach.com

Nursing Clothing and Accessories

Motherwear   800-950-2500 or www.motherwear.com

Breastfeeding Help and Resources

La Leche League International (LLLI) 800-435-8316 or 847-519-7730 or www.lalecheleague.org

International Lactation Consultant Association (ILCA) 919-787-5181 or www.ilca.org

Corporate Lactation Program by Medela 800-435-8316 or www.medela.com

Attachment Parenting International 615-298-4334 or www.attachmentparenting.org

Mothering Multiples

National Organization of Mothers of Twins Clubs, Inc. 877-540-2200 or 615-595-0936 or www.nomotc.org

Index